Two Million Silent Killings

This compassionate and hard-hitting book is the most robust and loving defence of the unborn child which I have read. It combines Christian orthodoxy, social caring, and medical knowledge which will be hard to refute by any theologian, sociologist or doctor who may resist its bold pro-life stance.

> *Bishop Maurice Wood, DSC, MA, RNR*
> *Chairman, Order of Christian Unity*
> *September 1986*

This book is rare. It is one of very few written by a campaigner involved in the fight against abortion from the beginning in 1966 and as such demonstrates an unusual depth of knowledge and insight into the fight. Margaret White is also one of the very few involved in the fight against abortion on both sides of the Atlantic and her book gives a comprehensive picture of the campaign in America (where she is invited regularly on lecture tours) as well as in the United Kingdom.

'It is a much needed and very necessary addition to pro-life bookshelves'.

> *Phyllis Bowman,*
> *National Director,*
> *Society for the Protection of Unborn Children.*
> *August 1986.*

Two Million Silent Killings

The Truth about Abortion

Margaret White

Marshall Pickering

Marshall Morgan and Scott
Marshall Pickering
3 Beggarwood Lane, Basingstoke, Hants RG23 7LP, UK

Reprinted: Impression No.
88 89 90 5 4 3 2

British Library CIP Data
White, Margaret
   Two million silent killings: the truth about abortion.
   1. Abortion——Religious aspects——
   Christianity
   I. Title
   261.8'3   HQ767.2

ISBN 0 551 01402 4

Text Set in Linotron Ehrhardt by Input Typesetting Ltd.,
London SW19 8DR
Printed in Great Britain by The Guernsey Press Co. Ltd.,
Guernsey, Channel Islands.

Photographs used are:
WITH PERMISSION, *Human Life & Abortion; The
Hard Questions*, Willke Hayes Publishing Company,
Inc., Cincinnati, OH, U.S.A.

Contents

1

What's All The Fuss About?

'Thus saith the Lord thy redeemer and he that formed thee from the womb; I am the Lord that maketh all things; that stretcheth forth the heavens alone; that spreadeth abroad the earth by myself; that frustrateth the tokens of the liars and maketh diviners mad.' *Isaiah 44. 24.*

I'm sure David Steel had the best intentions when he introduced his Private Member's Bill into the House of Commons in 1967. It was the tail end of the Swinging Sixties, the adolescents of those days were convinced that a brave new world of modern technology was just around the corner and all would be merry and bright. A popular slogan of the time, written on walls and hoardings was 'God is dead', and certainly a lot of people behaved as though He was. For the majority of people the only religion was materialism, and a whole generation grew up in the belief that possessions brought happiness. It was not surprising therefore, that there was a move to do away with laws which were considered to be merely relics of our bygone Christian past. Within a decade the laws were changed to make pornography and gambling legal, divorce easier to obtain, homosexuality acceptable behaviour and abortion available on demand. David Steel denied repeatedly that his Bill would permit abortion to become legal for anyone who had the money, for any reason or none and up to the seventh month of pregnancy. The Bill was called the Medical Termination of Pregnancy Bill and kept that name until it reached committee stage in the House of Lords. Their Lordships, seeing (what members of the lower House couldn't or wouldn't see) that abortion was going to have little to do with the great art of Medicine and a lot to do with killing the unborn, renamed it *The Abortion Bill*.

Probably few of the Members of Parliament who voted for the Bill had any idea what genie they were loosing from the bottle. MPs have to attend and vote in debates on such diverse things as the teaching of science and the government of a crown colony; they can't have deep knowledge of everything. Abortion is a subject about which it is very easy to be emotional, and the line taken in support of it was powerfully emotive: the 'agony' of the overburdened mother whose health would be ruined by yet another child. The 'overburdened mother' has never received so much attention from Parliament as she did during the Abortion Bill. Many a crocodile tear was shed over her desperate situation, and yet she disappeared from the scene almost as soon as the ink was dry. Within a very short time the figures showed that most abortions were performed on the *childless*, as they still are. The 'overburdened mother' had served her purpose to the abortionists and was thereafter forgotten. The other horror story with which Members of Parliament were regaled was the suffering of women who went to the back-street abortionists. The House was told perfectly true stories of women who had developed serious bleeding or infection following illegal abortions. In fact, though they still occurred, deaths from 'back-street' abortion had been going down rapidly for over fifty years, and even if they had not the solution proposed in the Bill was much the same as solving the drugs problem by issuing addicts with sterile syringes – an attack on the effects rather than the causes. A medically supervised injection of heroin will stop the addict catching hepatitis, but it will not help his addiction, and in exactly the same way the prevention of illegal abortion could not hope to reduce the incidence of abortion itself. That, of course, had never been the aim of the pro-abortion lobby that promoted the Bill.

And so the pass was sold. Effectively, society's weakest and most innocent members lost their right to be treated like the rest. Because their presence was inconvenient they were to be killed and thrown into a bin and burnt, and all with the blessing of the law. We are all distressed when someone dies in the prime of life, it is of course a tragedy, but at least they have lived for half their allotted span. The unborn child, like all of us made in the image of God and known by him is deprived of his entire life on earth. The Swinging Sixties have a lot to answer for.

In our materialistic society very few things are considered evil. The Ten Commandments have disappeared from the walls of most of our churches and are rarely taught to children or mentioned in schools. There is one evil that is condemned by everyone, however, and that is discrimination – either racial or sexual. This is no doubt due to the appalling revelations of the Nuremberg trials, when the world first learnt the full horror of the way the Jews had been treated in Nazi Germany. Racism and sexism are universally condemned because Christians and humanists alike both accept the principle that, whatever your race, shape, colour or sex, you are all part of the human race and entitled to equal rights and privileges. How odd that, while this belief has become stronger and more universal in the past twenty years, it has become possible for many people to believe equally strongly in their right to destroy a human being of any race and colour just because he is small or unwanted. Highly intelligent people, among them many Nobel Prize winners apparently cannot see the extraordinary contradiction in attacking discrimination with one hand and supporting it with the other.

Abortion in History

Abortion has been condemned as an evil not only by Christians and Jews, but by peoples of all religions and none. It has often been said by those who support abortion on demand, that it was only in the nineteenth century that abortion became illegal. In fact they are wrong by thirty-seven centuries. The first recorded law on abortion was in Sumeria in the 18th Century BC; we know it was considered a crime as long ago as that because the punishment is documented for both deliberately and accidentally causing an abortion. The Babylonians also have left a record from the 16th Century BC of the punishment for causing an abortion, as did Tigleth Pileser, King of Middle Assyria, whom we know of from the Old Testament.

The first mention of abortion in the Bible is in Exodus, Chapter 21, verse 22: 'If men strive and hurt a woman with child so that her fruit depart from her and yet no mischief follow, he shall be surely punished.' The Jewish moral code of the sixth century BC contains the phrase 'Nor shall the woman destroy the embryonic child in her womb'. These few examples make it perfectly clear that, just like thieving and murder, condemnation of abortion is not exclusively Christian. The earliest Christian reference to abortion comes in the second century AD in the *Didache* (also known as *Instructions to Apostles*). As a Christian expansion of Mosaic Law it is a wonderful set of rules for living. If only half the population of the world lived by them, most of the problems that beset us would melt away like the snow in spring. 'Thou shalt not kill; Thou shalt not commit adultery; Thou shalt not corrupt children; Thou shalt not commit fornication; Thou shalt not murder a child by abortion nor kill one after birth . . .'

Under English law abortion has always been a crime. A textbook of the law written around the year 1250 by Henry de Bracton, one of Henry III's judges, stated that abortion was the same as homicide. Throughout the centuries it continued to be a crime under common law and in 1809 a law was passed which made abortion punishable by being fined, imprisoned, put in the pillory, whipped or transported for up to fourteen years – a pretty hefty deterrent! This was altered by the *'Offences Against the Person' Act* of 1839, and again in 1861. This statute still governs the law today. It is important to realise that under the *Abortion Act* of 1967, abortion is still illegal, but exceptions are made so that, in certain cases only, there will be no prosecution. The law of 1861 laid down that any woman who took 'any poison or other noxious thing or shall unlawfully use any instrument or other means whatsoever with the like intent . . . shall be liable at the discretion of the court to be kept in penal servitude for life.' By the same Act it is an offence punishable by up to three years imprisonment 'to supply or procure poisons or instruments knowingly for the purpose of abortion'. In spite of this very strict law it was accepted by the courts in the early part of the twentieth century that an abortion could be performed in the very rare cases where this was necessary to save the life of the mother. Many doctors felt this was too strict a guideline and that abortion should be available if there was a serious risk to the physical health of the mother, and a few went even further and thought that risk to the mental health of the mother should also be grounds for an abortion. Dr Bourne, an eminent gynaecologist, was able to get the law altered by performing an abortion on a fourteen-year-old girl who had become pregnant after being raped by a number of soldiers. He told the police before he did it and invited arrest. It became a *cause célèbre* known as the 'girl and the guardsmen case'. Dr Bourne was duly brought before a court and charged with an illegal abortion. As the punishment was almost certain imprisonment and being struck off the medical register, it is possible to admire his courage, if not his actions. He pleaded that he feared for the girl's mental health, and was acquitted.

From 1939, the date of his acquittal, abortion to preserve the physical or mental health of a patient became legal.

The first countries to legalise abortion were the USSR and its East European satellites. In fact by 1967 when the British Abortion Act finally reached the statute book, several of these satellite countries were already unhappy with the number of abortions being carried out, far more than had been expected. This was not for religious reasons but because of damage to the health of women who had been aborted. Doctors in Czechoslovakia and Hungary published articles in the medical press on the serious physical and emotional complications that followed abortion. All of the communist powers were worried by the rapid reduction of population that followed the introduction of easily obtained abortion. (These facts were duly reported at the time of the debates in Parliament but received very little coverage in the press.) Japan, a small country always worried about over-population, was next to legalise abortion on demand. The first country in the west to permit abortion (except for serious risk to the life of the mother) was Sweden, a country that already enjoyed a reputation for being avant-garde in public morals and had a high incidence of divorce and suicide. The second country was Britain, which had at that time a low incidence of both.

The Determined Minority

It has often been said that 'History is made by determined minorities', and the legalisation of abortion is a perfect example of this. A tiny organisation of mainly humanists, with financial help from the Hopkins Fund of California, were able to get a member of Parliament to put forward, as a private member, a Bill legalising abortion under what were considered strict controls. That in itself was no mean feat. Members of Parliament had tried it before and failed to get the Bill passed. So the pro-abortion lobby tried a different tack, and convinced a large number of legislators that the Bill would not permit abortion on demand, but would merely make it a bit easier for doctors to help 'overburdened' mothers of large families, who though medically unfit to have another child couldn't have an abortion under the law as it stood. The pro-abortionists were skilful in getting good press coverage. The television was swamped with grisly stories of women dying from back-street abortions, the women's magazines dwelt on the need to change the law to make abortion easier because it was so necessary after rape. And although the medical profession, especially the gynaecologists, totally opposed any change in the law (as did the churches, lawyers and most women's organisations) in the end persistence paid off and the Bill was passed.

The Bill as it was finally passed read as follows: 'For the purposes of the law relating to abortion, anything done with intent to procure the miscarriage of a woman is unlawfully done unless authorised by Section 1 of this Act.' In Section 1 we find that: 'Subject to the provisions of this Section a person shall not be guilty of an offence under the law relating to abortion where a pregnancy is terminated by a registered medical practitioner if two registered medical practitioners are of the opinion formed in good faith a) That the continuance of the pregnancy would involve risk to the life of the pregnant woman or of injury to the physical or mental health of the pregnant woman or any existing children of her family greater than if the pregnancy were terminated or b) There is a substantial risk that if the child were born it would suffer from such physical or mental abnormalities as to be seriously handicapped.'

Most Members of Parliament who voted for the Bill did not believe it would permit abortion on demand. They were assured by the sponsor of the Bill, David Steel, that it would not do so. Yet within a few months of the Bill becoming law, London became the abortion capital of the world, taxi drivers were touting at airports and collecting desperate girls to take

7

them to private abortion chambers which had sprung up like mushrooms overnight.

The pro-abortionists admitted after the law was changed that they had got the Bill through Parliament by stressing the 'hard case'. There is no doubt that a lot of people were swayed by stories of over 100,000 back-street abortions being performed in Britain, causing death or permanent ill health to poor frightened women. In fact there were nowhere near 100,000 back-street abortions – this was a figure produced to shock and frighten. Because they were illegal it is impossible to know how many back-street abortions were carried out, but to judge from the figures for women who either died or were admitted to hospital after an illegal abortion, also from a paper published by the Royal College of Obstetricians and Gynaecologists (entitled Legalized Abortion: Report by the Council of the RCOG and published in the British Medical Journal of 2nd April 1966) it was only about 14,000. It is important to note that this figure included abortions carried out illegally by doctors operating in private clinics as well as those cases where women interfered with themselves, or were operated upon by back-street abortionists. This technique of inventing frightening figures for back-alley abortions has been used by abortionists all over Europe, and in spite of its obvious inaccuracy it works every time. It was used in Italy when pressure was successfully put on the government to alter the law. It was said that there were two million illegal abortions a year and 20,000 deaths. Not only would this ridiculous figure have meant that every woman in Italy, including nuns, would before long have had back-street abortions, but more women were alleged to have died from illegal abortions than the total number of deaths in that age group. A few years later the same technique worked in Portugal, again the figures were absurd, but they were believed. It was the Nazi Goebbels who said 'If you are going to tell a lie, tell a big one, and if you repeat it often enough most people will believe you.' This big lie was believed world-wide.

In the USA the law was altered not by the elected government, but by the appointed Supreme Court. They laid down that women had an absolute right to abortion up to the sixth month of pregnancy and for medical or psychological reasons up to nine months. Most other countries have some restrictions. In Canada there is a special committee in hospitals that approves or disapproves each case, though in many hospitals this is a farce as no case is refused. In France and Germany abortions may only be performed up to a certain stage of pregnancy. The law varies from country to country, but the effect has been that, throughout the whole 'Christian' world abortion has become more or less available on demand for the most trivial of reasons. It is now a fact that in the affluent west the most dangerous place for a child to be is in his mother's womb.

The Uncertain Trumpet

The change of law in the United States was not only the most extensive but also the least democratic. The situation there had varied from state to state, with California – the richest state of all – having abortions for all who could pay. California also had the highest divorce rate.

In January 1970 the Supreme Court, the non-elected defender and upholder of the Constitution, decided in the critical Roe v. Wade ruling that, because the Constitution granted individual privacy no-one had any right to forbid abortion. Later in 1976 they went even further and declared that a doctor need not provide the same medical care for a baby born alive after a late abortion as he would for a baby delivered in the same place after a normal confinement. It is hard to see how such blatant discrimination fits in with the rights given to citizens of the USA, of 'Life, Liberty and the Pursuit of Happiness'.

This somersaulting of the law on abortion throughout the western world would not have happened had there not been a considerable 'softening up' of the general public beforehand. Television was very powerful in the sixties and on it people were fed regular doses of 'situation ethics.' The line taken was: 'No one likes abortion, doctors hate doing it, but tragically it is absolutely necessary to prevent the greater evil of women dying from back-street abortions.' Later this was expressed in television dramas and films where young girls committed suicide because they were pregnant and couldn't get an abortion. (In fact a woman is less likely to kill herself when she is pregnant than at any other time in her life.) Programmes and articles were written explaining that unwanted children were more likely to become battered babies, or juvenile delinquents (again, quite untrue), so that people everywhere were saying to each other over their coffee cups 'Well, I don't approve of abortion, but it's better to have nice clean hospital operations than dirty back-street ones', in other words underwriting the old heresy that it is fine to do evil if you think that good may come of it. So the morally unthinkable of one generation becomes common in the next.

One of the tragedies of the abortion battle was the weak lead given by most of the Christian churches. There were some marvellous exceptions, but the most striking thing about most of the religious leaders was that they emulated Tar Baby and 'kept on saying nothing'. The Roman Catholic Church in Britain made a conscious decision to keep quiet because it did not want abortion to be labelled 'merely a Catholic issue'. The Church of England largely ignored the issue. There were never more than seven bishops in the House of Lords while it was being debated, and if any sermons were preached on the subject they were few and far between. Far too many of the clergy were afraid of being unpopular or annoying their congregations by tackling such subjects as chastity or abortion, and so they preached on the evils of poor housing, war, race and sex discrimination, or hunger. And yet St. Paul writes that significant sentence, 'If

10

the trumpet give an uncertain sound, who shall prepare himself to the battle?'

The change of the law in Britain allowing abortion acted like a card falling in a house of cards; one by one they tumbled and the last ones fell more quickly than the first. Throughout the western world countries rescinded their laws forbidding abortion: America, Canada, Australia, France, Germany, then the rest of Europe, so that at the time of writing Belgium and Portugal are the only countries in what might be called the developed world which do not have a law permitting abortion more or less on demand. The abortion holocaust had started; human life became cheap once more, and all because too few people in countries with a Christian heritage had had the courage to demand real facts and act in the cause of justice. As W. B. Yeats put it,

The ceremony of innocence is drowned.
The best lack all conviction while the worst
Are full of passionate intensity.

2

The Early Biography of Everyman

'Thine eyes did see my substance yet being imperfect, and in thy book all my members were written, which in continuance were fashioned when as yet there were none of them'. *Psalm 139: 16.*

'Thus saith the Lord thy redeemer and he that formed thee from the womb. I am the Lord that maketh all things.' *Isaiah 44: 24.*

Dehumanising the Young Human

In Ethiopia the word for 'pregnant' means 'she became two souls'. There's no confusion there as to what happens when a woman conceives. When my mother became pregnant my father told his friends and relatives 'my wife is with child'. I often wish that we had not exchanged those beautifully descriptive words for the cold, scientific and rather ugly-sounding 'pregnant'. The whole question of whether abortion is right or wrong stands or falls on the question of whether the child in the womb is a living member of the human race or not, and therefore whether abortion kills a human being. Those who support abortion do everything in their power to dehumanise the foetus; in fact there are two rules which are seldom forgotten when pro-abortion speakers are trained. The first is 'Never accord humanity to the foetus', and the second, for those who are going to debate with pro-lifers, is 'Don't let the pro-lifers show pictures'. As the object of those who support abortion on demand is to convince the general public that what is in the womb is nothing more than a 'shapeless mass of jelly', they do all in their power to prevent the truth of what is in the womb at the various stages of pregnancy becoming common knowledge.

It is, of course, impossible to deny that abortion kills living human beings, the unborn child has a human mother and a human father, and it is not necessary to be a professor of biology to know that the product of conception from two humans has to be human. The foetus is certainly alive before an abortion; if it were not alive there would be no need to do an abortion – the mother would miscarry. A common cause of miscarriage is where some defect in the sperm or ovum prevents the foetus developing normally, and it subsequently dies. The mother will then miscarry either at once or possibly some weeks later. When the miscarriage occurs some weeks after the death, it is called a 'missed abortion'. Technically the word 'abortion' means the premature termination of a pregnancy before twenty-eight weeks (after that it is called 'premature delivery'). This termination of pregnancy can either be medically induced or spontaneous. The causes of spontaneous abortion are many. The mother may lose her baby due to a defect in the baby, and this happens usually early in pregnancy where for some reason nature has 'boobed' and the child in the womb is quite incapable of independent life. Nature, having made the mistake, proceeds to put it right by causing the mother to miscarry. Alternatively the cause of an abortion may be a defect in the mother's womb. Damage to the neck of the womb from a previous surgical abortion can cause a miscarriage, as can fibroids (harmless tumours) in the womb. Dietary deficiency or problems with glands producing insufficient or excessive secretion of hormones can also cause the loss of a baby, even though the womb and the child are normal. These cases where the baby's loss is spontaneous are usually called 'miscarriage'. In popular parlance the word 'abortion' is reserved for induced abortion.

13

The belief in the humanity of the foetus is the basis for the pro-life position. Christians believe that the child in the womb is a child of God, and see each human being as unique and worthwhile. But for those who have no religion at all, even science itself shows that it is false to pretend the foetus is not, from the moment of conception, a separate human individual. Genetically the foetus must be a member of the human race because of his twenty-three pairs of chromosomes in every cell nucleus; likewise he can't be just a part of his mother or a part of his father, because these chromosomes are derived equally from both parents. It is extraordinary that, in spite of there being billions of people in this world, nowhere is it possible to find two 'identical' individuals. This remarkable fact, which shows the complete uniqueness of every human being, is due to the huge number of genes on the chromosomes and their remarkable diversity. Even 'identical' twins, which, because they both come from the same egg and sperm are remarkably alike in many ways, are nevertheless not identical – they do not, for instance, have the same fingerprints. From the moment of conception the child is a dynamic, rapidly growing individual – over nine months the single fertilised egg will grow into trillions of cells in the new born child.

Debating recently with a consultant gynaecologist I was shocked to hear him say 'The sperm is alive, the egg is alive, life is a continuum, there is no special time when life begins'. This amazing 'doublethink' can't be believed by anyone who has studied embryology, but it is often said to justify both abortion and the human vivisection of embryos for research purposes. The sperm and ovum are certainly alive, but once the egg has left the ovary and the sperm has left the testes, their life span is limited unless they meet and fuse. Both the egg and the sperm will have died a natural death a week after sexual intercourse unless conception occurs, but once the egg and sperm have fused, they become a new person who may well live for seventy years. The events that follow fertilisation are self-generated by the new individual, within a few days this tiny speck has moved from the fallopian tube where conception occurs, to the womb, where mother nature has provided a specially thick lining, well supplied with blood vessels to receive the fertilised egg. On arrival in the womb, the first action of the embryo is to burrow into the thick vascular lining specially prepared to receive it. If pregnancy does not occur there is no need for this thick lining, and so the body gets rid of it by menstruation. That is why menstruation is sometimes called 'the tears of disappointed pregnancy'. This settling down of the fertilised egg in the womb is known as 'implantation' – just as a mole will burrow into the lawn, this new being 'burrows' into the lining of the womb. So inbuilt is this burrowing action that it has been reported that embryos which were fertilised in a petri-dish, to implant into an infertile woman in the process of *in vitro* fertilisation, were left in the dish too long and tried to burrow (implant) into the dish!

The new combination of chromosomes present at conception sets in motion the life of the individual; he is controlled by his own code which is determined by the genes on the chromosomes. These genes contain a library of information from the past on the incredible helix of DNA (Desoxyribonucleic acid). A single thread of DNA from a human cell contains information equivalent to over half a million pages with five hundred words to a page, or a library containing a thousand volumes! The stored knowledge at conception in the new individual's 'library' is fifty times more than that contained in the entire *Encyclopaedia Britannica.* It is hard for us to comprehend the knowledge of a large library stored in that tiny new life, so small it can only just be seen with the naked eye.

Dr. Hymie Gordon, Chief Geneticist at the Mayo Clinic, put it thus: 'From the moment of fertilisation when the desoxyribo-nucleic acids from the spermatozoon and the ovum come together to form the zygote, the pattern of the individual's constitutional development is irrevocably determined; his future health, his future intellectual potential, even his future criminal proclivities are all dependent on the sequence of the purine and pyrimidine bases of the original set of DNA molecules of the unicellular (i.e. single cell) individual. True environmental influences, both during the intra-uterine period and after birth, modify the individual's constitution and continue to do so right until his death, but it is at conception that the individual's capacity to respond to these exogenous (i.e. from outside the body) influences is established. Even at that early stage, the complexity of the living cell is so great that it is beyond our comprehension. It is a privilege to be allowed to protect and nurture it.'

The Mere Fertilised Egg

Those who support abortion are very dismissive of the foetus, which, they claim, is not a real human being, but only a *potential* human. But this is just as ridiculous as disliking the dawn because it is only *potentially* a day. I am regularly accused of making an unreasonable amount of fuss about a 'mere fertilised egg', to which I reply that all of us, from dukes to dustmen, were 'mere fertilised eggs'. None of us 'came from' fertilised eggs any more than we 'came from' toddlers – we *were* once fertilised eggs just as we were once toddlers, and the fact that we don't remember being either doesn't make it any less true. We were just as human then as we are now: there is no essential difference. And I might add here that it takes only the slightest doubt of a distinction between the so-called potential human and the real thing to deal a fatal blow to the anti-abortionist's case. After all we do not bury those who are only *doubtfully* dead, or leave victims of an earthquake in the rubble because we *doubt* they are still alive. The only human way to behave is always to give life the benefit of the doubt.

In 1981 the Senate of the United States of America

considered a *Human Life Bill*. Senator John East chaired hearings for eight full days, during which they received personal testimony from fifty-seven witnesses, including national and international authorities. The official report included the following statement: 'Physicians, biologists and other scientists agree that conception marks the beginning of the life of a human being – a being that is alive and is a member of the human species. There is overwhelming agreement on this point in countless medical, biological and scientific writings'. On pages 7–9 of the report they list a small sample of thirteen medical text-books, all of which state categorically that the life of an individual human being begins at conception.

Since *in vitro* fertilisation has been used to overcome the problem of female infertility it has become even harder to deny that the embryo is a living human being. In this method of overcoming childlessness several eggs are taken directly from the mother's ovary and mixed with the father's sperm in a petri dish. When there are three embryos formed they are carefully put into the woman's womb from below. (The method is usually used to overcome an obstruction in the woman's fallopian tubes, which stops the sperm and egg meeting in the normal way.) No woman is going to pay large sums of money to a doctor, to insert into her uterus an embryo if it is not a living human being. Likewise no doctor would put a non-human or a dead embryo into a womb. Both affirm by their actions that the embryo is living and human. Many scientific studies agree with them. The September 1970 issue of *California Medicine* includes the sentence, 'It is a scientific fact that human life begins at conception and continues intra- or extra-uterine till death'. *Life* magazine, in a special issue, *The Drama of Life before Birth*, states 'The birth of a human really occurs at the moment the mother's egg is fertilised by one of the father's sperm cells'. In one way or another they point to what has long been accepted as fact in Chinese culture, where a child is considered to be a year old three months after birth.

Early Development of Everyman

How much time does it take to make a man? Napoleon said twenty years; philosophers say a lifetime; the Christian would add – eternity. By a long, long road of careful patient observation the doctor discovers an evident truth which everyday language has always recognised – man is never complete.

Implantation in the womb begins about a week after conception, when there are already several hundred cells present. Once Jemima has settled herself happily in the lining of the womb which we call the endometrium, she starts developing very quickly. (I'm calling my embryo by a name because I don't want her to be just an anonymous scientific detail, and because Jemima is the name I gave my first baby when I was pregnant – she was born prematurely and stillborn.) By seventeen days she has started to make blood cells and a day later a primitive heart is forming. This is at first just a bend in a tube which is an early blood vessel, but in spite of being only a primitive heart it is starting to beat at three weeks, and by the end of the first month it is beating regularly and smoothly, expanding and contracting. Some researchers have observed occasional contractions in the heart of a two-week old embryo.

We know Jemima is a girl, because four days after conception, with a special microscope, we can tell the sex. Before the heart starts to beat her nervous system has begun to develop, and by the end of the twentieth day the foundations for her brain, spinal cord and whole nervous system will have been laid down. Forty-two days after conception doctors can pick up her brain waves on the electro-encephalogram (EEG) and her nervous system will now be controlling the movements of her muscles and her heart, even though her mother may not yet be sure if she is pregnant or not. Jemima's eyes start to form about the same time as her heart. At first they look like black spots, almost like a panda. That is because what can be seen first is the retina, which very soon disappears to the back of the eyeball, to play the most important part in the mechanism of sight. Four weeks from conception she has the rudiments of forty pairs of muscles.

An awful lot happens in the first month of Jemima's life; she has completed the greatest physical change of her life. Never again will she grow so quickly. She is ten thousand times larger than she was at conception, and has grown from one cell to millions. From head to foot she is a quarter of an inch long, the size of a split pea. She has a head with primitive eyes, ears, mouth and brain, simple kidneys, a liver, a digestive tract, a primitive umbilical cord and a big heart (in proportion to the size of the body it is nine times as large as the adult heart). This heart pumps sixty-five times a minute to circulate the newly-formed blood through a system of tubes which are completely separate from her mother's circulation. The constantly increasing number of cells become different from each other and each takes on a specialised function. They need to be controlled properly so that they grow in the right place at the right speed. We do not know how this is organised, but biologists believe there is a chemical communication between different cells. Dr Corner, in his book *Ourselves Unborn* describes this rather well: 'Imagine a little workshop started by a man with all-round talents. His first employees learn the business from him and as the factory grows they become department heads, each organising his own part of the work until all sorts of specialised workers are developed, capable in their turn of developing new employees, but only in their own narrow fields.'

By the beginning of the second month she is beginning to look like what she is – a human. I say 'look' because since Professor Ian Donald of Glasgow University developed the old wartime technology of echo-sounding into ultra-sound scanning that is exactly what you can do, at least from about the eighth week of pregnancy. And the sight is stunning. In the first few days of the second month her arms, hands and the finger outlines can be seen, at five weeks the internal hearing apparatus is almost complete. The two ears develop simultaneously as do the hands and feet. What is interesting is that already the ears, hands and feet are showing a hereditary pattern; in a family with large and prominent ears, these can be seen in their offspring before the second month of pregnancy is over. By seven weeks from conception Jemima has become a well-proportioned small-scale baby – she could be described as a one-inch miniature doll with a slightly large head, slim arms and legs and an unmistakably human face. Her body is not a doll's body. Even the most expensive doll can do little more than say 'Mama' and 'suck' a bottle. Jemima's body works, her brain sends out impulses which co-ordinate the functions of the other organs; not only is her heart beating well but her stomach is producing digestive juices, her liver is making blood cells and her kidneys are excreting waste products. The muscles of the arms are working and jerky movements of the arms can be seen with ultra-sound scanning. The skeleton, though primitive, has been complete from six weeks.

At this stage all the unborn are especially vulnerable to outside influences, physical or chemical, because certain diseases of the mother can be passed on to the child, the most susceptible parts being, naturally, those that are growing most rapidly at the time of the mother's infection. The virus of German Measles (Rubella) affects different bits of the embryo, depending on the stage of the mother's pregnancy. Certain drugs, smoking, alcohol, radiation and (where the child is a boy) the contraception pill can all have an effect on the growing embryo in the first ten to twelve weeks of life.

After the eighth week, everything is already present that will be found in a full-term baby. From this time until adulthood, the changes in Jemima's body will be mainly in size and increased efficiency of the working parts.

In the third month Jemima becomes very active, though she still only weighs an ounce and could easily move around inside a goose's egg. By the end of the second month she is kicking and waving her arms and turning somersaults. This can be clearly seen on ultra-sound screening, and because she is surrounded by fluid she is almost weightless, and the kicks and 'head-over-heels' look like a child bouncing up and down on a trampoline. She can swallow and does so, drinking and later excreting the fluid in which she swims. We know that by the eleventh week of pregnancy her taste buds are perfectly formed and there are more of them than there will be after birth. In fact, never again will her taste be so good. We know that if we make the fluid sweeter by adding glucose, she will drink more, and if something that tastes unpleasant is added to the fluid she will taste it, grimace and wrinkle up her nose, looking for all the world like a child who's been given a teaspoonful of nasty medicine to take.

She has been able to feel pain since soon after the sixth week, but now the whole of her body is sensitive to touch. The back, top and sides of a baby's head remain totally insensitive till after birth. To be born, all babies have to push hard at the neck of the womb to help it to open, the top and sides of the head are squashed and moulded and, in some cases bruised by the normal birth process, it is an example of the miraculous nature of pregnancy that this one part of a baby's body has no sense of feeling, and therefore birth is not nearly as traumatic for babies as it would otherwise have been. If her eyelid is touched she will turn her head away and frown, if the palm of her hand is touched she will close her hand in a partial 'fist' (not till the fifth month will she be able to grip anything firmly, and this 'grasp reflex' lasts till some months after birth). In the third month she makes a discovery that her thumb is a pleasant thing to suck and throughout the rest of her intra-uterine life and for the first few years of her life after birth she will get comfort from thumb-sucking. She starts to 'breathe', not air of course, but she inhales and exhales the fluid in which she swims. By the end of the third month all babies start to demonstrate their own individuality, both in appearance and character. The muscles of Jemima's face follow an inherited pattern, and her facial expressions are already similar to those of her parents.

Further refinements that arrive in the third month are the fingernails and the vocal chords; also the sexual difference is obvious from both internal and external sex organs. Even more amazing, the primitive sperms and ova are already present in the sex glands, and at this stage also she starts to urinate. The fluid into which the baby urinates also acts as a protection, the child at three months is naturally fragile – as is the newborn baby – the fluid protects against most forms of accidents, occasionally it is unable to do so, but nature can even perform miracles here – if the child sustains a fractured limb due to a serious fall by the mother, the limb will heal naturally, even a gunshot wound which was once incurred at three months healed naturally, leaving only a scar at the time of birth.

The Growth Phase

In the fourth month Jemima really starts to grow, and her mother will begin to 'show' that she is pregnant, because her womb in the fourth month rises out of the pelvis and flops forward on to the abdominal wall. By the end of the month she may be startled one day to feel an odd 'tap tap' some- where below her umbilicus. If it's her first baby she may think it's just wind in her bowels, if she has already had one child she will know that this gentle 'tap tap' is her baby, who is now big enough for her kicks and punches to be felt. In four weeks Jemima gets six times heavier than she was and grows to half the height she will have at birth; she will be six to eight ounces in weight, and eight to ten inches tall. The heart can now be heard through the mother's abdominal wall, and is pumping up to six gallons of blood a day. For this prodigious growth the baby must take in a lot of nourishment; she needs food, oxygen and water, and she gets them from her mother through the placenta or 'after birth'. The name placenta comes from the Latin word for cake – this is apt as it is food for baby and looks like a primitive cake, round and rather flat. It used to be thought that most of the placenta was formed from the mother's tissues and only a little from the baby. We now know that the placenta (and the membranes, cord and amniotic fluid) are all formed from the original fertilised egg. The placenta is rooted in the lining of the womb and at four months is about three inches in diameter. At birth it will have grown to twelve inches in diameter and can weigh over a pound. It is a powerful organ which performs the functions of the adult lungs, kidneys, liver and bowels, and as well as that, produces substances that will give Jemima immunity to some infections.

Her blood flows into the placenta through the umbilical cord, but never meets her mother's blood (this is vital because she might have a different blood group to her mother). The exchange of her carbon-dioxide for her mother's oxygen, and her waste products for her mother's nutrients is carried out across the walls of the porous blood vessels. The placenta not only serves her but also her mother; it becomes the main source of the hormones necessary to her mother's body in pregnancy and to prepare for the production of milk. As well as hormones the placenta makes what are called 'Gamma Globulins'; these are a natural ingredient of the blood which give both mother and baby an increased resistance to disease. Jemima's blood is carried to the placenta by her umbilical cord; the blood stream in the cord travels at four miles an hour and completes the round trip through baby and cord in thirty seconds. The force of the blood within gives it the consistency of a well filled garden hose and so it resists the formation of knots and tangles.

Though there is no intermingling of the mother's and baby's blood, there are certain substances, potentially harmful to the baby, which can sneak through and damage the unborn child. When I was a young doctor working in obstetrics I was taught that the old idea that what the mother ate or drank might harm her baby was 'an old wives' tale'. The belief was that as long as a mother's body was adequately nourished, other things didn't matter. Now, after many a tear has been shed over a still-born or handicapped child, we know that an enormous number of things have an effect on the unborn child. Cigarette smoking increases the risk of a premature and undersized baby; alcohol affects babies' health, and the child of a heroin addict is born a heroin addict also. Deficiency in certain minerals which may be lacking in our twentieth century artificial diet can even cause miscarriage. The medical profession was very slow to realise a lot of these facts and it was mothers themselves who took the bull by the horns and founded an organisation called Foresight, which helps mothers to prepare themselves for pregnancy by using a diet which will protect the health of their baby.

The Fifth and Sixth Months

In the fifth month Jemima grows to be one foot long and weighs about a pound; her skeleton becomes a bit harder, as do her nails, but physically she alters little except to grow. Nearly all her development was done in the first few months. She already has her baby teeth in her gums, and in her sixth month she also gets her permanent teeth high up in the gums. Her grip is now perfect, and she can hold on tightly to something in her hand. A joke is told about the child of two expert pick-pockets who were very distressed when their baby was born with a clenched fist that no-one could open.

After some weeks they managed to pull back the clenched fingers when the baby was asleep, to discover clenched in her baby palm the midwife's wedding ring! Many a true tale is told in jest. Babies do clutch tightly from six months of intra-uterine life to six months after birth. This 'grasp reflex' is almost certainly implanted to help the child at the breast, for when the child is breast-feeding it clutches and pummels at the breast, so helping the milk to come through and the child to suck.

In the fifth month the baby starts to hiccough, something the mother will detect as a rhythmic jolting movement and the doctor as a clicking sound. In this month also the child gets to know and recognise its parents' voices. This is known because if a baby in the womb hears a strange sound, especially a loud one, her heart will beat more rapidly until she gets to hear the sound a few times, and then she recognises it and knows it is harmless. Many people have observed that new born babies will cry at the sound of a stranger's voice but never at their parents' because they have been listening to their voices for months and they know them. At six months Jemima can see light through the wall of her mother's womb when her mother is undressed or in a loose nightie.

At this point the baby could, with expert medical help, survive a premature birth, for an incubator is a good enough substitute for the womb to enable her to continue her growth. In fact in a country like Britain this is now a relatively common occurrence. But it is a sobering thought that in Britain as well a thousand babies of this age emerge from the womb not to go into the incubator, but to be dumped, often still kicking and breathing, in a dish which is then removed and placed in the sluice room. In this case the newborn child is regarded as not 'viable', and yet the only difference between this and the premature births lies not in the baby herself, but in the attitude of those responsible for her wellbeing.

The Ninth Month

By her two hundredth and sixtieth day Jemima stops growing. The placenta, her 'cake', has got old and is sending out chemical messages to her mother, which would within a week start her into labour. Jemima has lots of hair on her head and even on her body, though you couldn't see it on her body because it is covered, just like channel swimmers, with a white greasy substance called 'vernix'. She has long eyelashes and beautifully shaped eyebrows. She weighs about seven pounds and, after twisting and turning quite a lot to make herself comfortable, she settles into a position with her head down, her arms folded across her chest and her legs crossed. There is nothing left for her to do but wait for the drama of birth.

Since her parents conceived her, Jemima has grown from one cell to two hundred million, and she weighs six billion times more than the fertilised egg. Were she to continue to grow after birth as she did before, she would be twenty feet tall by the time her teens were over.

After the trauma of labour she finds herself in an environment a chilly twenty degrees colder than the womb; it's hardly surprising she opens her mouth and screams. She is upset also that, without the buoyancy of the fluid, she can't hold her head up, so she waves her arms and struggles. Someone kindly wraps her in a warm blanket and gives her to her mother, who clasps her to her breast. With her head against her mother's chest Jemima again hears her mother's heart beat. That is a sound she knows; she'd been listening to that heart for months, and to that familiar sound Jemima falls asleep.

3

The Medical Profession –
Tarnished Halos?

'Dispense true justice and practice kindness and compassion each to his brother, and do not oppress the widow or the orphan, the stranger or the poor, and do not devise evil in your heart against one another.' *Zechariah 7: 9–10*

'He that followeth after righteousness and mercy, findeth life, righteousness and honour.' *Proverbs 21: 21*

The Origins of Medical Ethics

In the first half of the twentieth century doctors were considered not only as members of a noble profession, but also as examples of people who were trying in a very practical way to carry out Our Lord's instruction 'Love they neighbour'. It is doubtful if they deserved such reputation, but it certainly existed. Tragically, it exists no more. Not only has the profession appeared over-concerned with financial rewards but patients have become worried about the way doctors do things. The fact is that medical students rarely receive instruction in ethics in medical schools, and the profession itself is not agreed on which ethics are valid and which are not. Most patients still feel trust in the family doctor they have known for years, but the situation is very different when they are confronted with hospital admission for a serious illness. The surgeon can look disconcertingly like a scientist, someone whose interest is less in you as a person than in your body as a piece of organic plumbing. What he is able to do with that body in the technological era is one thing that urges the public to seek reassurance about his motives in doing it. What, in short, are his *ethics*. It is a question people have been asking for a long time.

Before Hippocrates there were no physicians as we know them, only apothecaries. These were businessmen; they were knowledgeable about herbs and roots, and made pills and potions for all sorts of conditions and diseases. But they had no ethical code of any sort and so provided whatever drug their customers required – they would sell you a potion for a stomach upset as readily as a poison to kill your enemy, and if you got your prescription muddled it was too bad.

Hippocrates, the Father of Medicine, knew thoroughly that kindness and piety in a physician were not a substitute for knowledge, but as an educator he also knew (better than many doctors do today) that the intimate and complex relationship between a doctor and his patient necessitated something above and beyond the mere pinning on of a disease label and the writing of a medical prescription. This comprehension is obvious from his persistent concern for the whole of his patient. Psycho-somatic medicine was no mere specialisation for him. He knew, all those years ago, that a patient consisted inseparably of mind and body – a combination to which Christians would add a third component – the soul.

Hippocrates observed many significant facts about medicine that we forget today at our peril. For instance he noted that the art of medicine co-operates with nature, that it 'does for nature what nature would do for itself if it could'. He observed also that 'The gods are the real physicians, though people do not think so'. For Christians, the book of Nature was written by the first person of the Trinity, God the Father, who made heaven and earth and all that is in them, and according to Dr Ratner in the international medical journal *Child and Family*, medical educators with an insensitivity to the Hippocratic tradition and an ignorance of the Christian tradition, miss truth in a two-fold way. As a result, in these modern times when medical ethics are in a state of flux, 'Physicians are treating health as though it were a commodity to be bought rather than a state which should be sought through wise accommodation of one's own nature to nature, and a loving subjection of one's being to God'.

The Oath and After

'I swear by Apollo, physician by Aesculapius, by Health by Panacea and by all the Gods and Goddesses, making them my witnesses, that I will use treatment to help the sick according to my ability and judgement but never with a view to injury or wrongdoing. Neither will I administer a poison to anybody when asked to do so, nor will I suggest such a course. Similarly I will not give to a woman a pessary to cause abortion but I will keep pure and holy both my life and my art. I will not use the knife not even verily on sufferers from the stone, but I will give place to such as are craftsmen therein. Into whatsoever houses I enter I will enter to help the sick, and I will abstain from all intentional wrongdoing and harm, especially from abusing the bodies of man or woman, bond or free'.

Reduced to its bare essentials this means that a doctor promises to do his best for his patients, never to poison them, to know his limitations and refer to specialists cases he is not qualified to treat, not to do abortions, to lead a good life himself, and not to commit adultery with a patient.

Hippocrates revolutionised the healing art and it is a measure of his greatness that it is only in the twentieth century that his Oath has fallen into disuse. Throughout all these centuries the medical profession as a whole upheld Hippocratic principles, but in the early part of the twentieth

29

century a dangerous heresy was born – eugenics. It was particularly dangerous because the originators of the science had the best intentions and the principle behind eugenics was one that we could all applaud. It is defined in the dictionary as 'the science of the production of fine (especially human) offspring'. Yet in spite of its aim this science in certain hands became one of the most evil in history.

Hitler did not invent the fascist 'super-race' mentality – he inherited it. Germany, long before Hitler came to power, had been interested in the philosophy of Hegel, and its eugenic application. Hegelian philosophy was a sort of pragmatic utilitarianism: if an action provides a solution for a practical problem it is morally justifiable. In other words, you may do evil if you think the end result will be good. In 1931 before Hitler came to power, a meeting of psychiatrists in Bavaria discussed sterilisation of the unfit and euthanasia of persons with chronic mental illness. Germany was not alone in discussing the problem. Margaret Sanger, who founded Planned Parenthood in America, whose motto was 'More children from the fit and less from the unfit', received financial help from the Brush Foundation for Racial Purity, and in Britain one of the objects of the Eugenics Society in the early days was to prevent 'people of subnormal biological endowment' having children. Hitler only licked his finger to see which way the wind was blowing; when he found out he turned it into a whirlwind.

What is frightening is that he had so little difficulty in getting the help of the medical profession. Long before the war Hitler had managed to persuade doctors to send mentally handicapped children from the homes and institutions to be killed. Later the adult mentally ill were taken away to be killed, and doctors who had taken the Hippocratic Oath signed the death certificates of their patients before sending them off.

The change from caring to killing doctors was not rapid; it was a slow process and took several years. As well as

Hegelian philosophy and eugenic science a book written in 1920 had had an enormous influence. It was called *The release of the destruction of life, devoid of value*, and was written by a lawyer and senior psychiatrist called Alfred Hoche. The book makes a plea for the killing of worthless human beings, who represent 'a foreign body in human society.' (Much the same language was used by the pro-abortion lobby, when they were trying to get the law altered: in 1920 as in 1967 the economic factor was stressed.) The professor of psychiatry in Munich, Ernest Ruedin, was able to get a law passed in 1933 which allowed compulsory sterilisation for eugenic reasons and was the harbinger of the mass killings of mentally and physically handicapped patients. Professor Ruedin specifically warned psychiatrists against the 'excessive compassion and love of one's neighbour characteristic of past centuries'. Perhaps the most sinister aspect of this mass murder was that it was not compulsory in the early days; no doctor was penalised if he refused to work in these hospitals, and yet more than twelve university professors of psychiatry took part. The methods used for the killing varied: carbon-monoxide gas chambers, starvation, injections of morphine, and, for the children, usually barbiturate or chloral poisoning. For several years during the time of the exterminations psychiatrists held meetings under the chairmanship of the professor at Heidelberg to discuss the relative efficiency of the methods.

Complicity went far beyond the doctors actually responsible for the deaths. One professor of pathology who did not take an active part in the killings nonetheless arranged to receive the brains of victims. He was given six hundred brains by the end of the war and claimed to have done valuable research on them. Another type of inhumane research was carried out to find the most suitable protective clothing for German pilots shot down over a cold North Sea in winter, and for this adult males would be issued with various types of clothing and then immersed in ice cold water while someone recorded how long it took them to die. The eugenic prin-

31

ciples justifying this sort of outrage were taught freely in German schools. Even the abstract subject of mathematics was not immune, for problems set for children required them to compare the cost of new housing for married couples with that of maintaining geriatric patients in hospitals.

Before the new values of Nazism the morality of the medical profession collapsed like a house of cards. Only in the Netherlands did doctors receiving a command from the Reich Commisar – to report incurably ill patients for extermination – actually dare to disobey. Their reward for this was the removal of their licences. Later a hundred of the country's leading doctors were arrested and sent to prison camps in Germany. But they never betrayed the Hippocratic Oath, and Holland became the only occupied country whose medical profession stayed true to its principles.

To all these atrocities the German authorities gave neat euphemistic labels. For instance, the buses that took the physically and mentally handicapped to the killing centres were presented as the *Charitable Transport Company for the Sick*. And the extermination camps themselves were run by an organisation called the *Realms Committee for Scientific Approach to Severe Illness*. It was a sad indictment of the sciences in Europe that mere extermination should have been called scientific.

The New Hippocratic Oath

After the Nuremberg trials the whole world was shocked at the horrors that were revealed of the mass murder of the Jews. Less attention was paid to the mass murder of the mentally and physically handicapped. It became clear at the trials that not only the hopelessly retarded had been destroyed, but even children with minor deformities or who wet their beds. The medical professions in Europe and America decided that such an appalling prostitution of medicine must never happen again, and in 1947 the World

32

Medical Association was founded, following discussion with the medical associations of all the countries in the United Nations. The British Medical Association submitted a very powerful statement to the World Medical Association in June 1947, entitled *War Crimes and Medicine*. It is worth quoting.

The evidence given in the trials of medical war criminals has shocked the medical profession of the world. These trials have shown that the doctors who were guilty of these crimes against humanity lacked both the moral and professional conscience that is to be expected of members of this honourable profession. They departed from the traditional medical ethic which maintains the value and sanctity of every individual human being.

Crimes committed by doctors have been classified by the War Crimes Commission as follows:-

(1) Experiments without consent on human subjects authorised by high authorities on the pretext of scientific research in the interests of the war.

(2) Experiments without consent conducted by medical officials in concentration camps on their own initiative in order to gain experience.

(3) Deliberate selection and killing of prisoners in camps by medical neglect or by lethal injections.

(4) Deliberate killing of infirm or feeble-minded patients and of children in hospitals and asylums.

From the above it is clear that doctors carried out their inhuman experiments both for the furtherance of the war effort and for research in disease. In the course of the experiments and in the application of their findings, they deliberately killed persons politically undesirable to the regime in power. They misused their medical knowledge and prostituted scientific research. They ignored the sanctity and importance of human life, exploiting human beings both as individuals and in the mass. They betrayed the trust society had placed in them as a profession.

The doctors who took part in these deeds did not become criminals in a moment. Their amoral methods were the result of training and conditioning to regard science as an instrument in the hands of the State to be applied in any way desired by its rulers. It is to be assumed that initially they did not realise that the ideas of those who held political power would lead to the denial of the fundamental values on which Medicine is based.

Whatever the causes such crimes must never be allowed to recur. Research in Medicine as well as its practice must never be separated from eternal moral values. Doctors must be quick to point out to their fellow members of society the likely consequences of policies that degrade or deny fundamental human rights. The profession must be vigilant to observe and to combat developments which might again ensnare its members and debase the high purpose of its ideals. The medical crimes committed in the late war have shown only too convincingly how medical knowledge and progress, unless governed by humanitarian motives, may become the instruments of wanton destruction in the pursuit of war.

The influence of Medicine throughout a nation is often under-estimated. Individually the doctor is more than the exponent of medical opinion and the technical expert. He is the confidant, the friend and the trusted adviser, and wields an influence far beyond the immediate realm of physical needs. Collectively the medical profession can cultivate throughout the world the growth of international amity.

The following procedure by the World Medical Association is accordingly recommended:-

(1) The publication of a resolution endorsing judicial action by which members of the medical profession who shared in war crimes are punished.

(2) The drafting of a World Charter of Medicine. This might take the form of a modern affirmation of the

aims and ethics of Medicine in the spirit of the Hippocratic Oath, which should be published and applied in medical education and medical practice.

In medical education, the traditional aims and ethics of Medicine should pervade the curriculum. An undertaking to abide by these principles as expressed in a Charter of Medicine should be part of the medical graduation ceremony.

In medical practice, the adoption of the Charter by the World Medical Association and its constituent bodies, and publicity through the world medical Press, would do much to prevent a recurrence of such crimes and to ensure that Medicine remains a constructive and beneficent influence in society as a whole.

The statement also included two appendices, given as follows:

APPENDIX 1.
Summary of medical crimes, abstracted from reports of Nuremberg Trials 1945–46.

An abstract of the available evidence indicates that the so-called experiments include:

(a) The effect of vacuum and pressure chambers.
(b) Sterilisation – chemical, operative, and radiological, with controls by artificial insemination.
(c) Blood transfusion.
(d) Cold water immersion, with periodic blood tests and different methods of resuscitation.
(e) Liver puncture.
(f) Deliberate septic infection.
(g) Excision of parts of the body.
(h) Experimental operative surgery – non-indicated operations – for instructional purposes.
(i) Exposure to gas and chemicals for varying periods and results checked by autopsy.

35

(j) Methods of 'mercy killing', gas, benzene injections, cremation of semi-moribund individuals before death, etc.

APPENDIX II

Principles for inclusion in a Charter of Medicine

AIMS. The traditional aim of Medicine has been the succour of the bodily needs of the individual irrespective of class or race or creed, the cure of disease, the relief of suffering, and the prolongation of human life. In later years the prevention of disease has been added to the traditional aim. All these have been accomplished by the scientific method coupled with the spirit of charity and service.

The achievement of the highest possible level of health for all people is an aim of the World Medical Association.

ETHICS. Although there have been many changes in Medicine, the spirit of the Hippocratic Oath cannot change and can be reaffirmed by the profession. It enjoins;

The brotherhood of medical men.

The motive of service for the good of patients.

The duty of curing, the greatest crime being co-operation in the destruction of life by murder, suicide, and abortion.

Purity of living and honourable dealing.

Professional secrecy for the protection of patients.

Dissemination of medical knowledge and discovery for the benefit of mankind.

As can be seen the profession, in its principles for a Charter of Medicine includes the phrase 'The greatest crime being co-operation in the destruction of life by murder, suicide and abortion.' A year later the World Medical Association produced an important Declaration of Medical Ethics to which all countries in the United Nations assented. It was called the Declaration of Geneva. Amongst the many declarations it includes the promise 'I will have the utmost respect for human life from the moment of conception. Even under threat I will not use my medical knowledge contrary to the laws of humanity'.

Doctors throughout the world were able to sit back and heave a sigh of relief and say to themselves, 'Thank God the profession has cleansed itself from its appallingly unethical behaviour, and that it can never happen again'.

Back on the Slippery Slope

But the corruptions of the Nazi era, by proving that the unthinkable could actually be done, cast a long shadow forward.

Chloral, the sedative drug used for extermination by the Nazis, was used again in Britain during the seventies and killed the handicapped newborn that surgeons decided weren't worth operating on. What is significant here is not the use of the same drug, but the thin end of the wedge of discrimination between the human being that is worth preserving and the one that is not. In the case of a virtually inoperable and fatal deformity the decision as to whether the child should live may be out of the surgeon's hands; but can the same be said of the embryo that modern tests have shown to have Downs syndrome? The answer is no. With the aid of modern technology and training the Downs syndrome child can not only live but lead a happy life. Excusing an abortion on the grounds of preventing suffering either to the child or his parents thus turns out to be a whitewash on the same grim wall of positive discrimination erected by Nazi eugenics.

Of course the Nazis used euphemisms to cover their tracks, and so do we. 'Terminating a pregnancy' sounds a lot better than 'abortion', and both, for the pro-abortionist, are preferable to 'feticide' or simply 'murder'. But this issue is wider than abortion. Before the British Medical Ethics Committee stepped in with its new guidelines it was quite common for a doctor who decided against operating on a spina bifida child to ensure, by starvation or sedatives, that the child never got home, and this was justified as an act of compassion and described – again euphemistically – as 'letting nature take its course'. A better description might have been 'assisting the termination of the natural struggle for life.'

It is also erroneous to pretend that since doctors put the horrors of the Nazi era behind them they have stuck faithfully to absolute moral principles. Quite the opposite, for in the tight corners of modern medical practice ethical standards have tended to give ground to expediency, not the other way round. In this abortion is a prime example. At first, when the upheavals of the sixties brought a demand from humanists and women's rights campaigners that the law should be altered, the British Medical Association agreed that abortion should be made more easily available, but only where there was a genuine risk to the mother's health and where there was good reason to believe the child would be born seriously handicapped. They did not support the Abortion Act of 1967 which allows abortion for social reasons, and passed a resolution in 1968 opposing this aspect of the abortion law. In 1969 they complained about the way the Act was working. By 1975, however, there were no more qualms and by 1977 a resolution was passed supporting the 1967 Abortion Act which they believed was working well. Within ten years the medical profession had changed its position from opposing easily obtained abortion to supporting it, and the consultant gynaecologists who had opposed change in 1967 had completely reversed their position and – with honourable exceptions – toed the party line. Some were quite happy to make public announcements on television that they would do an abortion on any woman who wanted one.

The Abortion Act specifically included a conscience clause, stating that no one would be forced to perform an abortion against his conscience. But here the real evil of the change came into play, for the clause was effectively countermanded by the Chief Medical Officer of Health to the Ministry, who sent a letter to all the hospital boards with instructions that they must not appoint a gynaecologist unless 'he or she is prepared to do abortions where there is a demand.' By this simple method the Ministry of Health has ensured that a pro-life doctor would not get an appointment as a gynaecologist, and that abortion would be easily access-ible to whoever wanted it.

World professional bodies have done no better; the World Medical Association which was formed to preserve a high standard of medical ethics promptly altered the wording of the Declaration of Geneva when it became obvious that the desire for easy abortion had become sufficiently widespread. (One exception was the Muslim countries, who still permit abortion except where there is a risk to the life of the mother.) By changing the Declaration from 'I will have the utmost respect for human life from the moment of conception' to 'I will have the utmost respect for human life from its begin-ning', they were able to pretend a respect for human life and in the same breath permit abortion up to nine months. They were able to do this because doctors and scientists, though they know perfectly well that a new and unique human being is present when the egg and sperm unite (and all the diction-aries and text books give this as the start of life), insist that no one knows when life begins. Suggestions vary from implantation (when the embryo settles down in the lining of the womb and starts to form the placenta) to three or four years after birth, when the child can communicate properly with those around and becomes a 'socialised' being!

It should not be thought that all doctors approved of the situation where abortion was available on demand either for anyone with money enough to pay the private fee, or – as is now the case – in most National Health Service hospitals. The majority did not like the situation and knew it to be

39

wrong. A Gallup Poll postal survey of all practising gynae-cologists was done in the autumn of 1979. Over fifty per cent (more than 600) filled in the questionnaire. Only eight per cent of them were in favour of abortion on demand; but seventy-one per cent had performed abortions in the past month and fifty-three per cent had done so in the past week. Though the law in Britain does not permit abortion on demand, eighty-three per cent said it was in fact available on demand, and over half said they personally performed abortions in National Health Service hospitals – not because they believed it was right to do so, but because of pressure put on them. Fifty-four per cent of these doctors feared that if they refused to do abortions they would jeopardise their chances of promotion. Eighty-three per cent agreed wholly or partly with the statement 'Termination of pregnancy even in the early weeks is neither simple nor safe'. Ninety-three per cent agreed wholly or partly with the statement when it applied to abortion in the second three months of pregnancy.

The Declaration of Geneva, to which all doctors are bound, includes the phrase 'even under threat I will not use my medical knowledge contrary to the laws of humanity'. In 1979 gynaecologists were prepared to admit in a question-naire that they committed acts which went against their consciences because of 'pressures'. When Christ was born in Bethlehem, the civilised world as it was known then, was under Roman rule. This harsh rule permitted appalling cruelty to children, Christianity turned this anti-child philos-ophy upside down. To the Romans the born child and the child in the womb were part of their goods and chattels to be used as they wished. To the Christians the child was precious because of Jesus' saying 'Inasmuch as you did it to the least of these my little ones, you did it unto me'. This seems to have been forgotten by far too many members of my profession.

As always there is a remnant that remains. The World Federation of Doctors who Respect Human Life, founded in Holland in 1974 by delegates from only nine countries, now has nearly a quarter of a million doctors from thirty three countries as members, they are determined to be salt that has not lost its seasoning.

'Behold the days come saith the Lord God, that I will send a famine in the land. Not a famine for bread nor a thirst for water – but of hearing the words of the Lord'. *Amos. Chapter 9:11.*

4

Killing: The Right to Choose

'Even so it is not the will of your Father which is in
heaven that one of these little ones should perish'.
Matthew 18: 14

Almighty Father, whose son Jesus Christ has taught us
that what we do for the least of our brethren we do also
for Him, give us the will to be the servants of others as
he was the servant of all, who gave up his life and died
for us but is alive and reigns with you and the Holy
Spirit, one God now and forever. *Collect for Pentecost 11
(ASB)*

The American Experience

In 1859 in Louisville, Kentucky, the American Medical
Association held a conference on criminal abortion and
received a report from a committee it had set up two years
previously. It starts as follows: 'The heinous guilt of criminal
abortion, however viewed by the community, is everywhere
acknowledged by medical men'. It suggested that part of the
cause of abortion was 'a belief even among the mothers
themselves that the foetus is not alive until after the period
of quickening'. The final paragraph sums up their feelings
most forcibly – 'The committee would advise this body,
representing as it does the physicians of the land, publicly to
express its abhorrence of the unnatural and now rapidly
increasing crime of abortion, that it avow its true nature as
no simple offence against public morality and decency, no

mere misdemeanour, no attempt upon the life of the mother, but the wanton and murderous destruction of her child, and that while it would in no wise transcend its legitimate province or invade the precincts of the law, the association recommend by memorial to the governors and legislators of the several States and as representing the federal district to the President and Congress, a careful examination and revision of the statutory, and of so much of the common law as relates to this crime. For we hold it to be a thing deserving all hate and detestation, that a man in his very original (sic) whiles he is framed, whiles he is enlivened, should be put to death under the very hands and in the shop of Nature'.

It is interesting to compare this declaration of the American doctors in the last century with the declaration of the British Medical Association in its evidence to the World Medical Association in 1947. The language is different but the meaning is the same, both are lamenting the decline from the traditional high standards of medical care and insisting on a return to morality. The report was accepted by the American Medical Association which unanimously adopted a resolution which condemned 'the act of producing abortion at every period of gestation except as necessary for preserving the life of either mother or child'.

It is as well to remember that in the eighteen-fifties the United States was not the rich country it is now. People were poor, families were large and work was hard, and yet they abhorred and abominated abortion. Development brought a change of heart.

After 1967 the different States passed laws which mostly allowed abortion, but for very restricted reasons; in June 1970 New York passed a law permitting abortion on demand up to twenty-four weeks. But it was not until 22nd January 1973 that the Supreme Court struck down all laws against abortion and legalised it in all the fifty states throughout the entire nine months of a pregnancy. To do an abortion today in the last three months of pregnancy it is only necessary for one physician to deem it necessary for the mother's 'health', and as the Court defined health as 'physical, emotional, psychological and the relevance of the mother's age', there are few women who could not prove themselves eligible.

Slaves or People?

The reason given by the Supreme Court for this volte-face was that under the Constitution the unborn child was not a person, but the property of the mother. Many historians have noticed the resemblance of this judgement with the Dred Scott decision of March 6th, 1857, when the Supreme Court ruled once and for all that black people were not legal 'persons' according to the US Constitution and therefore could be enslaved, owned, bought, sold, used or even killed at the owner's discretion. Just like a decision by the Law Lords after a referral from the Appeal Court in the United Kingdom, that decision was final; the Supreme Court is the highest court in the land.

Those of us who fight for the right of the unborn child to live, are frequently accused of forcing our morality on others. We are attacked as interfering busybodies. The argument runs like this: 'Nobody is forcing *you* to have an abortion: I'm prepared to let you have the freedom not to have an abortion, why won't you let the rest of us, who don't share your Victorian morality, have the same right to choose as you have?' Put like that it sounds very reasonable. Geraldine Ferarro, when she was running for Vice-President of the United States, repeatedly stated that, though as a practising Catholic she would never have an abortion, she wouldn't dream of interfering with the right of anyone else to have one. But those who fought to free the slaves were also accused of being a lunatic fringe who tried to interfere with other people's civil liberties – the argument used against them ran like this: 'Nobody is forcing *you* to keep slaves, you have freedom of conscience to keep them or not, why don't you let the rest of us who don't share your puritan morality, have the freedom to choose?' In that garb the same argument looks very different.

Slavery was called by many 'a necessary evil' – an expression that today is regularly used to describe abortion. What people must realise is that necessary evils after a time come to be considered to be more and more necessary and less and less evil. In the nineteenth century when Lord Shaftesbury brought in a Bill to forbid the employment of small children in the coal mines he was attacked in a similar manner. Particularly interesting are the allegations made by the rich mine owners at the time, because they echo the attacks of today on those who seek to alter the permissive abortion law. Lord Shaftesbury, for instance, was assured by the experts of the time that these children did not suffer because they were not able to *feel;* it was said that the economy would collapse if children were not allowed to go down the mines, because the mineowners couldn't afford to pay wages for adults; and it was repeated *ad nauseam* that the reformers were being emotive and irrational and that their arguments produced plenty of heat but no light. Of course Shaftesbury was right. So was Wilberforce. And those of us who have been privileged to debate on abortion are well used to exactly the same 'arguments' being thrown at us in practically the same words (only now it is the foetus, not the child, who 'can't feel'). It very soon becomes clear that the critics' real objection has to do with the curtailment of their freedom.

Freedom is important. But all of us have limitations to our freedom. The law that forbids us to drive at more than thirty miles an hour in a built-up area, might be said to be forcing someone else's morality on us; but society has a duty to lay down laws on everything from over-loading a lorry to murder. Otherwise one man's freedom becomes another man's injustice. The question then is not whether freedom should be limited, but whether a particular limitation is justified, given

45

the effect of that freedom on others. And since abortion means the freedom to kill other human beings there is every reason to stop it by law.

A New Ethic for Medicine and Society

That is the heading over a leading article in the official journal of the California Medical Association, *California Medicine*, in September 1970. Throughout the western world the medical profession had been turned upside-down by the complete change in the traditional ethic of the sanctity of human life – this editorial describes the turmoil caused by this relatively sudden change in belief. It starts: 'The traditional western ethic has always placed great emphasis on the intrinsic worth and equal value of every human life regardless of its stage or condition.' After describing the new philosophy that what really counts is the 'quality' of life, it continues: 'It will become necessary and acceptable to place relative rather than absolute values on such things as human lives. The process of eroding the old ethic and substituting the new has already begun. It may be seen most clearly in changing attitudes towards human abortion. In defiance of the long-held ethic of intrinsic and equal value for every human life regardless of its stage, condition or status, abortion is becoming accepted by society as a moral right and even necessary. Since the old ethic has not yet been fully displaced it has been necessary to separate the idea of abortion from the idea of killing, which continues to be socially abhorrent. The result has been a curious avoidance of the scientific fact, which everyone really knows, that human life begins at conception and is continuous, whether intra- or extra-uterine till death. The very considerable semantic gymnastics which are required to rationalise abortion as anything but taking human life, would be ludicrous if they were not often put forth under socially impeccable auspices. It is suggested that this schizophrenic sort of subterfuge is necessary because while a new ethic is being accepted the old one has not yet been rejected'.

In other words it's necessary for doctors to lie like hell about what's in the womb, because people are still too squeamish about killing the innocent. But there are more arguments against tightening the abortion laws than the refusal to equate abortion with killing.

The Woman's Right to Choose

This is probably the commonest argument used by the pro-abortion lobby, who consequently regard themselves as 'pro-choice'. They will often go further and angrily reject any suggestion that they are pro-abortion, and insist they consider abortion to be always a tragedy, though because it is entirely a matter for the mother she must be given free choice to keep or destroy her child. After all, the child is part of her body and she has the right to do what she likes with that.

But this argument contains inaccuracies and several downright lies. Of course women have the right to choose what they do with their own bodies, but that freedom is not absolute. If they were to go out into the middle of town and strip off their clothes, they would soon discover they did not have the right to parade naked in the city centre. Nor do they have the right to chop off their fingers or their toes. Were they to do so it would not be long before they were under psychiatric care. Nobody has the right to shout 'Fire!' in a crowded cinema or sing bawdy songs at a meeting of the town council. They may think these restrictions unreasonable; the point is that the fact a body is *ours* does not entitle us, in general, to do what we want with it.

But even granted total freedom to use and abuse your body, it does not follow that the baby you carry is *part* of it. True, for the first nine months of its life the child lives inside the mother; he even taps into her blood supply indirectly and steals her oxygen and nourishment, but he is merely a lodger,

47

he has one room in the house and the landlady, so to speak, provides him with supper and breakfast. The child in the womb is no more part of the mother than the lodger is part of the dining-room wall. This is very simple to prove, for how could a male child be part of his mother's body? There is no such thing in this world as a human being who is partly female and partly male. It is impossible because in every nucleus of every cell of the female is a female X chromosome and in every nucleus of every cell of the male is a male Y chromosome. It is just as impossible to be a 'little bit male' as it is to be a 'little bit pregnant'. But what of a *female* child in the womb, can't she be part of the mother? Not at all. She may have the same sex, but she may also have her father's blood group, and it is impossible for a human being to have one type of blood in most of the body and a totally different blood group in another.

There are many other factors which prove it is impossible for the unborn child to be part of his mother's body. We are all different genetically, and even more fascinating, we are all different immunologically. So much so that forensic scientists have discovered they can use our unique immunological picture as well as our fingerprints. It has always been a mystery to embryologists why the woman did not 'reject' the child in the womb, just as she would react vigorously were she given a transfusion with blood that was not of her blood group. Nature, partly due to the amazing construction of the placenta and partly by means we do not understand, has endowed the pregnant woman with the ability to carry and nurture a child instead of treating it as a foreign body.

Feminists contend that the right to be born is exclusively derived from the *mother*. But it takes two to make a baby. The father of the child, even if he is not married to the mother, can be brought to court and an affiliation order sought that will force him to pay a sum of money every week for sixteen years to support his child. In marriage the father is responsible for the child's behaviour and his debts; if there

48

is a divorce the father is ordered by the courts to pay out child support until the child is sixteen (in certain cases eighteen). Yet according to the feminists he has no rights before his child is actually born; no matter how much he longs for a child he is powerless to stop his wife using his money to pay a doctor to kill the foetus. I doubt if the feminists would accept such an unjust situation were the sexes reversed.

The woman has the right to choose indubitably. She has the right to choose whether to have sexual intercourse, she has the right to choose whether to use efficient contraception, but once she is pregnant then she does not have the right to kill. The parents contribute only one cell each; nature does the rest. The parents are incapable of determining which egg fuses with which sperm, they do not develop and determine their offspring, that is done by nature and the God of nature.

But What about Rape?

I once did a phone-in ('open-line' in the USA) in Canada, which lasted an hour and a half. They obviously don't vet the questioners so carefully over there, because I was asked this question by five different callers. Rape is something that obsesses a lot of ordinary people. Twenty years ago I was able to answer with truth that rape was so rare in Britain that it was of no significance. Sadly I can do that no longer. At a time when there has never been more promiscuous and precocious sexual activity, when it has never been easier for a man to have a casual sexual relationship, vicious and violent rape of women and children has never been more common. It is hard to understand why, when we are going through what Malcolm Muggeridge has called a 'copulation explosion', it should be necessary for men to use violence to obtain sexual gratification. The answer may well lie with the women's movement. Rape is not the action of a sex starved man; rape is an expression of hate and loathing. The rapist does

49

everything in his power to demean and debase the woman, sometimes even to the extent of urinating over her. It is possible that this is the reaction of an inadequate man to what he sees as the aggressiveness of modern women which has robbed him of his masculinity. This theory certainly fits in with the picture of powerful and successful career women so frequently portrayed in magazines and on television – the number of such women has increased at about the same rate as the crime of rape.

The answer I gave to all the questioners on the phone was simple – Why should you kill an unborn child because it has a rotten father? You do not wipe out the violence of the rape by the violence of killing. It is impossible to be 'un-raped'. The plea to legalise abortion has always leaned heavily on the argument that we must have easily available abortion because of rape. In Britain abortion for rape has been legal since the thirties, but in spite of that, every attempt to tighten up the Act of 1967 provokes cries of 'What about rape?' One of the things I said to those five telephone callers in Canada was 'If abortion were only legal for rape or the life of the mother, I wouldn't be here, I'd be home in England with my husband'.

In fact the number of abortions for rape is still miniscule, way below one per cent. It is in fact very rare for women to get pregnant as a result of rape. The reasons are many: the woman may be on the pill, she may be too young or too old, and even if she is not taking the pill the rape may be during her 'safe' period. Even where a woman is raped during her most fertile period (the twelfth to fifteenth day before the first day of her next period) the terror of the rape may psychologically stop her ovulating. She may be sterile. Finally and by no means the least common, the man may function inadequately and there may be little penetration and little in the way of emission.

It is vital that any woman who is raped goes straight to hospital, because if she is treated at once with spermicide she will almost certainly not conceive. As long ago as 1971 the *Journal of the American Medical Association* reported that a survey of a thousand rape victims who were treated immediately afterwards showed not a single pregnancy. In 1977 a text book of Obstetrics and Gynaecology reported a series of one hundred and seventeen rape victims, of whom only seventeen were given hormone treatment, but none became pregnant. It does happen, but it is very rare and a very bad reason to permit the millions of abortions that are performed for quite different reasons.

Better avoid the Back-street

For medical personnel and politicians this is probably the strongest argument in favour of a permissive abortion law. It is true that in the past women suffered serious haemorrhage, infection and occasionally death after illegal abortion. But it is also true that women suffer haemorrhage, infection and death after legal abortion, so it is a question of numbers.

Those who support abortion on demand claim that deaths due to abortion have declined because of the Abortion Act which came into operation in April 1968. They certainly have declined, but this bears absolutely no relationship to the change in law. Many years before the Act abortion deaths had been dropping dramatically in England and Wales (as in every other country in the developed world) regardless of whether abortion was legal or not. The reason was the enormous advance that had been made in medicine, chiefly in the use of antibiotics and blood transfusions. In England and Wales deaths from abortion dropped from sixty-five in 1955 to thirty-two in 1967. After abortion became legal the deaths from abortion actually went *up* to thirty-five in 1969, falling to seven in 1976, rising to thirteen in 1980 and then going down steadily to six in 1984. Between 1955 and 1984 all deaths associated with pregnancy and childbirth (maternal deaths) went down from 439 to fifty-two, a very similar drop.

51

In Scotland there were no abortion deaths anyway in 1967, and in Northern Ireland the Abortion Act does not apply. Doctors there still do a very occasional abortion when they believe the mother's life may be in danger, but this has not produced a mass removal to dangerous back-street clinics. In fact abortion deaths have fluctuated between one a year and none for the past ten years.

The fact seems to be that abortion deaths were virtually a thing of the past before abortion was legalised in Britain. In Southern Ireland direct abortion is not allowed under any circumstances (indirect abortion is permitted when the mother has cancer of the womb or an ectopic pregnancy). In spite of this very strict law, abortion deaths are extremely rare. As far back as 1965 there was not a single death during the year from abortion, since then the numbers have fluctuated between none and two.

Of course we cannot be certain how many illegal abortions are performed now or were performed twenty years ago, any more than we know how many people steal from shops. We only know the number that are caught stealing, and we only know the number of women who die from illegal abortions. One thing *is* certain, the figures for abortion deaths used by the pro-abortionists are not only false, but what is more, they *know* they are false. Dr. Bernard Nathanson, who was a founder of the American pro-abortion organisation 'National Association for the Repeal of the Abortion Laws' (NARAL) wrote as follows in his book 'Aborting America 1979', describing how the law was changed in the United States to become the most liberal in the world – 'How many deaths were we talking about when abortion was illegal? In NARAL we generally emphasised the frame of the individual case, not the mass statistics, but when we spoke of the latter it was always 5,000 to 10,000 deaths a year. I confess I knew the figures were totally false and I suppose the others did too if they stopped to think of it. But in the morality of our revolution it was a *useful* (italics Nathanson) figure, widely accepted, so why go out of our way to correct it with honest statistics? The over-riding concern was to get the laws eliminated and anything reasonable that had to be done was permissible'.

The story in the United States was exactly the same as in European countries. The same scare stories were told about back-alley abortion deaths. In fact deaths there from abortion (spontaneous as well as illegal) were over fourteen hundred in 1941, but dropped dramatically as soon as penicillin became widely available, and were down to two hundred in the fifties. Before the Supreme Court decision which made abortion available on demand, the number of deaths were under sixty (a very good figure when compared with England and Wales. In spite of a population three times as great, and at that time no free National Health Service the deaths from abortion were only twice that of Britain). The most remarkable thing about the graph of abortion deaths in the United States is that, as in Britain, the drop in deaths is negligible after the law was passed making all abortions legal, compared to the drop before. Figures from countries as different in culture and religion as Portugal, Japan, France and Germany tell the same story. Deaths from abortion dropped enormously long before any law was passed making it legal. They have continued to drop since laws liberalising abortion were passed, but not by any means at an accelerated rate.

On the contrary there is good evidence that more liberal abortion laws actually increase the number of back-street abortions. In Japan in 1955 when abortion was available on request and as many as 1,170,1441 legal abortions were performed, the Japanese Ministry of Health estimated that at least 300,000 illegal abortions were performed as well. Christopher Tietze of the Population Council of America and a well-known pro-abortionist admitted that 'Criminal abortion and self-abortion have not disappeared even in Hungary, where abortion has been available on request for a decade'. Furthermore, a lot of abortions done before abortion became legal in both Britain and the United States were not back-street at all. Before the law was liberalised the patients went to the private clinics and handed over their cash, and the abortion was performed just as it is now. The difference was in the paperwork. Now the doctor will quite frankly write on the appropriate form 'Unwanted Cyesis – T.O.P.' (That is 'abortionese' for aborting for unwanted pregnancy.) Formerly they would write much more carefully and quite untruthfully that they suspected this lady had something wrong in her uterus and they were forced to scrape out the lining of the womb to discover what it was. There were, and still are self-induced abortions (usually by douching with soapy water) but abortions from untrained 'butchers' were rare. In the United States Dr. Mary Calderone, president of Planned Parenthood, said in 1960 in the *American Journal of Health* that 'ninety per cent of all illegal abortions are presently done by physicians'.

In 1978 against great opposition, Congressman Henry Hyde, one of the world's greatest fighters for life, pushed through Congress an amendment to cut off government funding for social abortions. In 1977 the United States government had paid for 295,000 such abortions on poor women. In 1978 it only paid for 2,000. There were dire predictions from medical statisticians that there would be at least seventy-seven extra deaths in women who would turn to illegal 'back-street' abortionists. They proved to be completely wrong; and a report from the Centre for Disease Control of the United States Department of Health and Welfare in February 1979 was forced to admit that 'No increase in abortion-related complications was observed. . . . No abortion deaths related to either legal or illegal abortions were detected'. In fact total maternal abortion deaths were actually lower than before the cut-off in 1976.

It is important to realise the significance of this statistic. There was a reduction of 293,000 legal abortions in one year, but an improvement in the death rate from abortion.

Many kindly Christian people are constrained to support abortion against their better judgement because they believe it will cut down on maternal deaths. But it hasn't: it doesn't, and it never will.

The Rich can Always Buy Abortions

An argument used widely to support a liberal abortion law runs like this: 'The rich have always been able to afford a private abortion, but the poor could not. It is the duty of a caring government to ensure that the poor have the same medical care as the rich'. Were abortion a totally good thing with good effects on the mother and child, and society, it would undoubtedly be right for the poor to have equal access to abortion with the rich. But abortion is not in the least beneficent; it is bad for the mother, fatal for the child, and has a debilitating effect on society as a whole. Because some rich women indulge in bad practices it is not beholden on the state to provide similar bad practices for the poor. The rich can also afford to buy drugs like cocaine or heroin, but this is no reason for making them freely available to the poor. Furthermore, there is someone who has been left out of this argument altogether – the victim.

It makes no difference if the mother is rich or poor; the child ends up dead, and there is no right so important as the right of life. So seriously do all people take this that capital punishment is being abandoned in more and more countries, people are opposed to war, and drunken drivers are severely punished because they might kill someone on the road. Surely an equally important way of obtaining justice would be to stop the killing of the child in the womb, because his mother, whether rich or poor, is alive and equality demands that the child be allowed to live also? A child has the right to be born because he is a child of the Universe and the God who directs its powers. No less than the trees and the stars he has a right to be here. He is innocent, and both parents and society have a duty to protect all that is human, especially the innocent.

Stopping the Unwanted Child

When I was nine years old I came home from school and found my mother weeping inconsolably. I was very upset and tried to comfort her. She told me she was going to have a baby and we couldn't possibly afford a fifth child, especially as the youngest, Jean, was only just over a year. If ever anyone was unwanted at three months, it was my younger brother, but he became without any doubt the most adored child. Baby Jean died of pneumonia when my mother was about seven months pregnant. From his birth until my mother's death, my younger brother was her greatest joy, and the most wanted person in the world. I give this personal story as an example of the fact that most unwanted pregnancies become wanted babies – just as some wanted pregnancies become unwanted babies. The first three months of pregnancy, when most abortions are done, is the worst stage of pregnancy to be making important decisions. It is true that in the last three months of pregnancy women are heavy and ungainly, but it is in its early stages that pregnancy has an effect on the emotions of women. This is the stage when a woman feels sick a lot of the time, doesn't fancy her food and bursts into tears at the drop of a hat. Her moods change from day to day. This is definitely not the time to be making life and death decisions, and to suggest that because a woman doesn't want a baby at ten weeks she won't want it at twenty, is, in many cases, incorrect.

There is something very sinister about the concept of the wanted child; it suggests that our right to be in this world depends on whether we are wanted or not. If we accept that, it is but a short step to saying we have no right to *stay* in this world if we are *not* wanted. I could make out a good case for quietly disposing of a drunken, dirty and diseased old man, deserted by his family and friends, lying on a park bench snoring, with a half-empty bottle of methylated spirits in his hand and the lice crawling over his face. Everything that is said in favour of killing the unborn can be said about him. In fact he has even less right to life then the child in the womb because he has at least been allowed to live to adulthood and it's his own fault he's in this state, whereas the child in the womb is not to be allowed into the world at all, and, unlike the drunk is completely innocent. Yet no Christian has any doubts that our duty is to do everything in our power to help this old man for the sake of our Father in heaven who loves him. Mother Theresa, who takes in the pathetic (and sometimes revolting) wrecks of human beings from the streets of Calcutta, and washes and feeds them so that they may die with dignity, has said 'There is no such thing as an unwanted child, if no one else in the world wants them – I do, you can send them all to me'.

But that will not be necessary, because there *is* no such thing as an unwanted child. There may be unwanting parents, but for every parent who does not want a child there are a hundred pairs of outstretched arms longing to receive it. The sex and the colour don't matter at all, nor does it matter if the child is handicapped, there are people throughout the country who are anxious to adopt a handicapped child. In the eyes of God the value of a human being does not depend on whether they are wanted or not, or perfect or not, but on the fact that they are made in the image of God and loved by Him. The slogan 'Every child is a wanted child' is dishonestly incomplete because what it means is 'if the child is not wanted it may be killed'. It is a rather primitive form of philosophy to suggest that problems can be solved by killing. We could solve the famine problem by killing off all the people who live in the areas where famine is endemic, and we could easily rid the world of leprosy if we killed all lepers.

But won't an unwanted child be an unhappy one? It is often claimed that unwanted babies become battered babies, juvenile delinquents, kids who do badly at school. But I do not see the logic behind battering a baby in the womb to prevent it being battered outside the womb. All of these gloomy predictions do not stand up to the light of day. Particularly significant is the work by Professor Lenoski, of the University of Southern California, who studied 674 battered children and compared with them a control group of children who had not been harmed. He found to his surprise that ninety-one per cent of the children who had been assaulted by their parents had been planned, compared with sixty-three per cent for the control group. They had obviously been very much wanted because the mothers of the 'battered' babies went into maternity clothes sooner than the control group, and the fathers named the boys after themselves four times as often as the control group.

Aborting babies does not reduce child abuse. In Britain the number of cases of serious cruelty to young children has increased since abortion became easily available, in Ontario there were 16,172 abortions in 1971 and 422 cases of child abuse, by 1978 there were 38,782 abortions and 1,762 cases of child abuse. In New York City the numbers of cases of child abuse rose from 5,000 a year before legalised abortion to 25,000 in 1975 after. In the United States as a whole, child abuse cases were 167,000 in 1973 and 929,000 in 1982. It would seem that the acceptance of the violence of killing the unborn, lowers parental resistance to violence towards the born. In Japan where abortion on demand has been available for thirty-six years, cases of infanticide have increased so much that the government is seriously worried. Particularly distressing is the cruel way the babies are killed, such as being thrown from the window of a moving train, or even more horrifying, being locked in a coin-locker and left to die.

The increase in the number of battered babies throughout the world shows that abortion is not a private act affecting no one but the mother and child. Where abortion is easily

A six week embryo. It is possible to discern head, fingers and eyes.

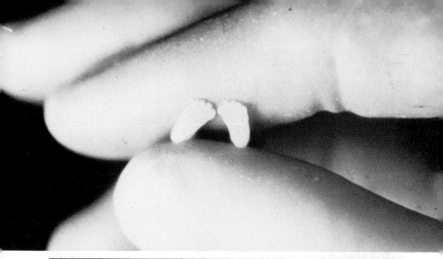

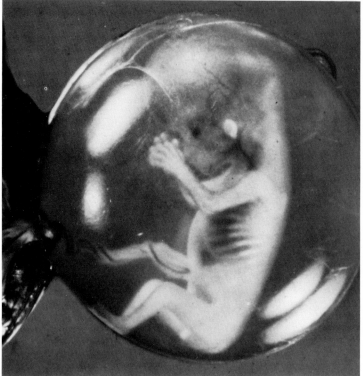

Top: The feet of a ten week foetus.
Bottom: 'Here I am in my bubble – a bit like an astronaut – I'm only eight weeks old.'

(Both pictures reproduced with permission of Willke Hayes Publishing Co. Inc.)

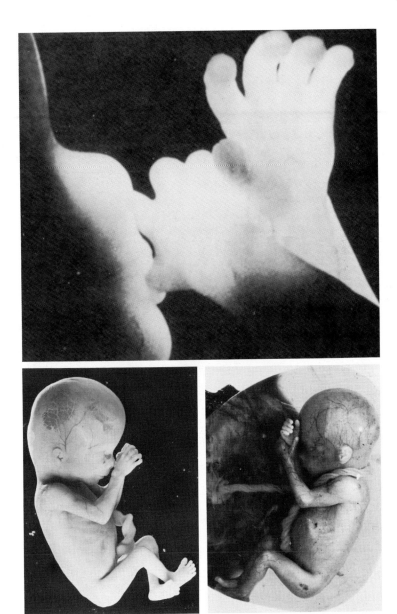

Top: Sucking his thumb, a foetus of about 3 months, 60 millimetres long.
Bottom: Both these unborn babies were killed at fourteen weeks old. Their only crime was being 'inconvenient'.

(Left: Reproduced with permission of the S.P.U.C. Right: Reproduced with permission of Willke Hayes Publishing Co. Inc.)

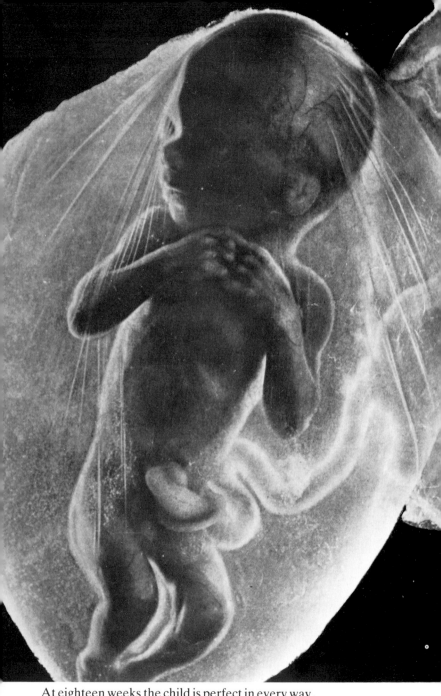

At eighteen weeks the child is perfect in every way.

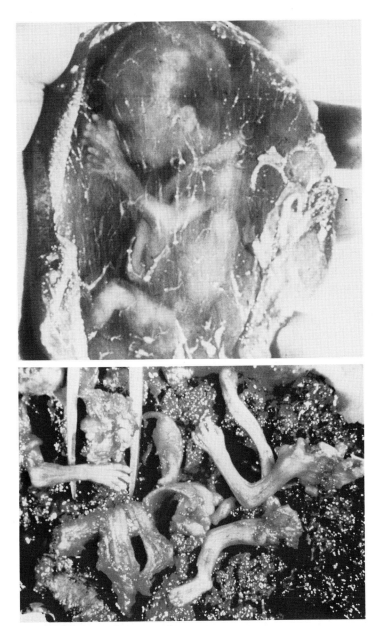

Top: A foetus at eleven weeks.
Bottom: The fruits of abortion — what a suction curette does to an unborn child.

(Both pictures reproduced with permission of Willke Hayes Publishing Co. Inc.)

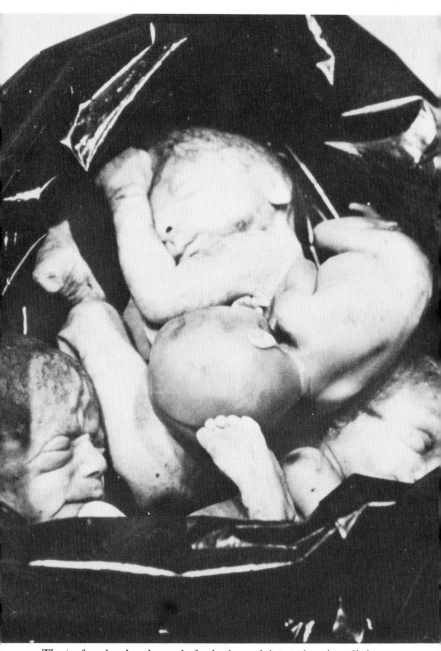

The 'refuse bag' at the end of a day's work in an abortion clinic.
(Reproduced with permission of Willke Hayes Publishing Co. Inc.)

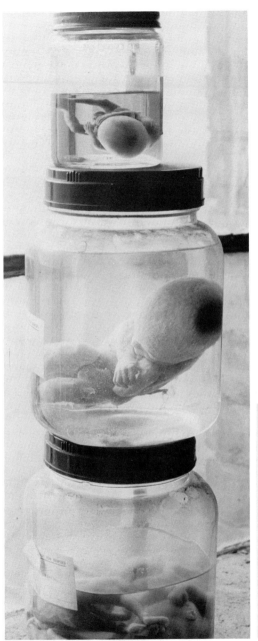

Embryos preserved in bottles.

A child from a primary school in Florida presents the author with a red rose, the symbol of the American pro-life movement.

available it has a profound effect upon the whole ethos of the country. There is a tendency to look upon human life as cheap and disposable, especially if that life comes into one of the despised categories such as unwanted, handicapped, old, senile, a nuisance. The logical conclusion of those who believe that the turbulent future of the unwanted child can be avoided by aborting it, is that all disabilities and unpleasant deaths can be eradicated by discontinuing the human race.

5

Death Before Birth

'These six things doth the Lord hate, yea, seven are an abomination unto him: A proud look, a lying tongue and hands that shed innocent blood, an heart that deviseth wicked imaginations, feet that be swift in running to mischief, a false witness that speaketh lies and he that soweth discord among brethren.' *Proverbs 6: 16 – 19*

Every three minutes, night and day, seven days a week a new life is ended by abortion in Great Britain. In the United States an unborn child is killed every thirty seconds. This mass slaughter of the innocents in Britain and America alone, omitting the millions of abortions done in the rest of the world, far exceeds the number of deaths caused by World War II, including the victims of air raids and the mass murder of Jews in Hitler's extermination camps. Unfortunately there are no cameramen in the womb to film the death and dismemberment of the unborn. Those who believe that abortion is a woman's right, naturally play down the seriousness of the operation and its after-effects. The world at large is constantly being told that to have an abortion is no more dangerous than to have a tooth out. But the fallacy of this point of view is underlined by the fact that large numbers of women who have suffered through abortion have formed an organisation, started in America, called Women Exploited by Abortion, or WEBA. One of their aims is to let it be known what abortion really involves.

Abortion – How it's done

There are three main methods of abortion. By far the commonest is invasion of the womb from below; the other two methods are the use of a drug to cause premature labour (the drug may include a poison which kills the child also), and surgical opening of the uterus and removal of the baby.

For the first few years after abortion was legalised the usual method was the first, an operation called dilatation and curettage. This operation is usually done, in the west, under a general anaesthetic; not so in the third world, where a local anaesthetic into the neck of the womb is all that is given. In order to get the baby out, it is necessary to get an instrument into the womb, and to do this it is necessary to open the neck of the womb (the cervical canal). Because nature cares very much about reproduction this canal is tightly closed. In order to open it instruments called 'dilators' are used – these start at a very small size and after the smallest has been inserted, the next size up is pushed up the canal until a dilator of ten to twelve millimetres will go easily into the stretched opening. While the canal is being stretched the neck of the womb is held by a toothed forceps. Once the neck of the womb is wide enough open, a loop-shaped steel knife called a curette is inserted into the cavity of the womb. With this sharp knife the abortionist cuts the baby and placenta into bits and scrapes them out into a bucket. The baby in this case comes out in quite big bits, and there can be a lot of bleeding.

Early abortions now are usually done by what is called 'vacuum aspiration'. The advantage of this for the mother (there is none for the child, who always ends up dead) is that the neck of the womb does not need to be dilated so much, because the catheter used is thinner than the curette and an opening of eight millimetres is usually enough. When the catheter is inserted into the cavity of the womb, one end of it is attached to a suction pump. This works on exactly the

61

same principle as a hoover but its suction power is twenty-five times as great. The catheter's end looks like a shark's mouth and is razor sharp. The suction is turned on and the catheter moved around inside the uterus and turned around from left to right and back again. The suction tears the baby's body into very small pieces which are pulled down a tube into a bottle. Because the pieces are small it looks as though there is nothing in the suction bottle but blood. This makes the operation much less objectionable for the nurses and doctors, because although they know exactly what they are doing, not being able to see the result makes it easier on the conscience.

Neither of these methods of abortion should be used where the woman is over three months pregnant, for the baby is too large to pass through the neck of the womb, even in bits. Even after ten weeks the baby's head is often too large and too hard to come out with the other bits of the body. The abortionist must always have ready a special forceps with looped ends. This he will put into the womb after the evacuation to grab the baby's head, which is then crushed by the blades of the forceps and removed.

Where a pregnancy has lasted for more than three months but less than five, abortion is sometimes done by a method called Dilatation and Evacuation. This is a particularly revolting method which even the doctors find unpleasant. Because the baby is a good size, the neck of the womb must be much more widely opened than with the other two methods. To make this easier it is quite common to put a special plug (called a 'tent') into the cervix the night before. This absorbs fluid and swells up, thereby slowly opening the mouth of the womb. The next day at operation the stretching is completed and an instrument like a pair of pliers is put into the womb. The ordinary curette or suction catheter are no good because the baby's bones have become much harder. With the pliers the baby is torn limb from limb and pulled out in pieces. The skull is crushed, as it is much too large and too firm to be pulled out intact. It is the unpleasant duty of the nurse to assemble the broken parts of the body, to be sure that no pieces are left behind in the womb.

Drug Abortions

The first drug abortion widely used was salt poisoning. This method is not used until the pregnancy is sixteen weeks or over. Using a syringe and a very long needle, a strong brine is injected into the amniotic fluid (the 'waters' that surround the baby). At this stage of the baby's development everything is present and all that is necessary is for the baby to grow. The skin, however, is still very thin and sensitive. Anyone who has ever accidentally put a scratched finger into some salt will know how painful it can be. Imagine the agony for this tiny human being, with its delicate skin and eyes, being completely surrounded with a strong solution of salt. The baby kicks and struggles violently, sometimes has convulsions, but in the end, inevitably, suffers an agonising death. After that the mother will go into labour naturally and be delivered of a child covered with skin burns from the salt, and with red eyes. The appearance of such a baby strikingly resembles that of children killed by napalm in the Vietnam war.

Because of the serious risk to the health of the mother, saline abortion is rarely used in Britain, though it is still common in the United States and parts of Europe.

The other common method of terminating a well-advanced pregnancy is by using the drug prostaglandin. This was produced by the American drug firm Upjohn and was approved officially for the termination of pregnancy between three and six months. It can be given like saline, directly into the amniotic fluid that surrounds the baby, or intramuscularly. More recently it has become available as a pessary to be put into the vagina. The action of the drug is to cause a contraction of the muscles of the womb, thus inducing premature labour. This can be extremely painful because the contractions are not those of a normal labour – in that case the baby is ready to be born and the neck of the womb waiting to open to permit birth; but these contractions are forcing a reluctant baby out of its natural home past a closed cervical canal, which does not want to open.

In most cases of prostaglandin abortion the baby is born alive. The World Health Organisation definition of a live birth is where the baby at birth shows a heart beat, or any attempt to breathe, or a pulsating umbilical cord, or any movement other than a twitch. Because they are very premature at four or five months the babies, though legally alive, will die within minutes. The problem arises when this method is used for a late abortion. After twenty-four weeks the baby is not only born alive but may be crying, and has a good chance of survival if he is taken to a special premature baby nursery. This causes a problem, for the object of the abortion was not to protect the health of the mother but to get rid of the child. So serious is this dilemma that some doctors, when they are injecting prostaglandin into the amniotic fluid, add a poison just to kill the baby. I have heard it said by gynaecologists that a woman who comes for an abortion has asked for a dead baby, and therefore it is the doctor's duty to see she gets one. In Orange County, California, a Dr. Waddell performed a drug abortion on a young girl, and when she was in labour went home. But she delivered more quickly than he had expected and the baby was alive, so the nurse took the baby and put it in an incubator, and sent for Dr Cornelsen, the children's specialist. When the abortionist returned he was furious to find the child alive and being cared for. He sent the nurse out of the premature nursery and in front of Dr Cornelsen strangled the child. The child specialist reported the case to the police who ordered a post-mortem. The coroner reported death by manual strangulation. But at the trial the defence lawyers insisted that, since abortion consisted of killing the unborn, the doctor was entitled by law to finish if off 'after the foetus was expelled from the womb'. Furthermore, they said, it did not make sense that what was perfectly legal within the womb became murder an hour later outside the womb. The doctor was acquitted.

In comparison to the use of prostaglandin, surgical abortions, where the baby is removed by an operation identical to a Caesarean section, are very rare. The difference is that with a 'caesar' as light an anaesthetic as possible is given so as not to affect the baby, whereas with an abortion they want a deeply anaesthetised baby, as it is less likely to live. This is a major operation and carries all the risks of major surgery. It is seldom used now because prostaglandin is easier and safer, but of course it presents similar problems to the surgeon. A recent headline in the *Obstetrics and Gynaecology News* read as follows: 'Live births main complication of midtrimester abortion'. What sort of society is it that considers the birth of a living child a 'complication'?

Therapeutic Abortion

Until 1967 all abortions were 'therapeutic' abortion. That means that their reason was to save the life of the mother, or because continuation of the pregnancy constituted a severe risk to her health. If a mother's life is threatened by pregnancy a good doctor will try to save both, and it is only very occasionally that a doctor really must kill the baby to save the mother's life. Some people consider surgery for an ectopic pregnancy to be an abortion. This is not so. An ectopic pregnancy is where the embryo never reaches the womb, but settles down and starts to grow in the fallopian tube. Because the muscle wall of the fallopian tube is not thick enough, after a few weeks the tube bursts because of the growth of the baby. Sometimes there is serious haemorrhage. This is called a 'ruptured ectopic' and is the most serious acute emergency in gynaecology. It is important to diagnose an ectopic pregnancy before it ruptures so that the pregnancy in the tube can be removed before it happens.

Where a pregnant woman is found to have cancer of the womb or some other equally serious condition, it is vital to do everything possible to cure the mother – if possible the baby should be saved, but the prime object of treatment must always be to save the life of the mother. If it is necessary to remove the uterus, baby and all, this must be done. The fact that the baby is killed does not make this an abortion, because killing the baby is not the object of the operation. The object is to save the life of the mother.

Complications and Side-Effects of Abortion

Every operation has a mortality rate, that means that there is a risk of death attached to all operations. In most cases the risk is small, in some surgical procedures such as heart transplants, the risk is considerable. The risk of death following abortion is small; the official record given for England and Wales is that one woman will die for approximately every twenty thousand abortions. This is a very low risk and many people might dismiss it as negligible. But we do not in fact know how many women die from abortion, because statistics depend on what is written on the death certificate – thus a woman's death may be certified correctly as due to an embolus (a clot that lodges in an important blood vessel), but the embolus might not have occurred had she not had an abortion ten days previously. Or death may be correctly certified as due to bronchopneumonia, but the patient would not have developed bronchopneumonia had she not had a general anaesthetic for her abortion. Therefore, though it is true that the death rate for abortion is low throughout the developed world, it is not as low as it appears to be from the official statistics. Doctors who derive considerable sums of money from doing abortions are not going to certify the cause of death to be due to abortion if they can find anything else they can legally put on the death certificate.

It is often said by those who support abortion that it is always safer for the health of a woman to have an abortion than to have a normal birth. They base this argument on the fact that the death rate for childbirth is greater than the death rate for abortion. But the women who die in normal childbirth usually die because they were already in a high-risk group. They had perhaps, diabetes, kidney disease, raised blood pressure, or an abnormality in the pregnancy or childbirth experience which could not be treated. There is no evidence that the deaths of most women who die in childbirth could have been prevented had they been aborted. And conversely, the overwhelming majority of women who die from a legal abortion are perfectly healthy before their lethal surgery and would not have died had they carried their babies to term. So no valid comparison can be made between these two groups of women. The death of a healthy woman from abortion is totally preventable by simply not aborting. In 1976 an editorial in the *British Medical Journal* contained the sentence 'In England and Wales abortion remains the most common cause of death associated with pregnancy'. In the *American Journal of Obstetrics and Gynaecology* in February 1978 we read: 'There has been no major impact on the number of women dying from abortion in the United States since liberalised abortion was introduced. . . . Legal abortion is now the leading cause of abortion-related maternal deaths in the United States'.

Another argument used in favour of abortion is the totally spurious one that childbirth is more risky for the girl under seventeen than for older women. Again this can be 'proved' statistically. I had always found these statistics surprising because my own personal experience was the reverse. One of the easiest deliveries I ever attended was that of a mother of only thirteen years old. I delivered many mothers under sixteen and all were trouble free. The answer to the apparent paradox lies in the ante-natal care these girls receive. We have known for decades that where there was little or no ante-natal care given, trouble could be expected at delivery; ante-natal care is a vital part of obstetric practice. Children under seventeen are usually pregnant outside marriage, and often try to conceal their pregnancy. This is sometimes because they are ashamed; sometimes because they just hope that if they ignore it, it will go away, and, undoubtedly, sometimes because they do not want to be pressurised by their parents or lover into having an abortion. It may be six months after they conceived before they finally reach an ante-natal clinic, and that is much too late. Many doctors in the past few years have surveyed childbirth in young women and all have reported that where the girl received adequate ante-natal care the young girl fares no worse than her older sisters. It was reported from John Hopkins University in 1975: 'With optimal care the outcome of adolescent pregnancy can be as successful as the outcome of non-adolescent pregnancy'. The *New York Times* on April 24th 1979, quoting the *Journal of Youth and Adolescence*, echoed my experience by reporting: 'We have found that teenage mothers, given proper care, have the least complications in childbirth. The younger the mother the better the birth'.

The Causes of Death Following Abortion

The causes of death following abortion are manifold, but the two main causes are haemorrhage and infection. The haemorrhage can be due to the catheter cutting into the uterine artery; infection is often caused by a small piece of the placenta or baby being left behind in the uterus. Sometimes pieces of bone which have been smashed by the abortion, instead of being sucked out of the womb, pierce into the muscle and become embedded. The patient is, in these cases, at double risk of haemorrhage and infection. It is not by any means a rare occurrence for the abortionist to push the vacuum aspirator right through the muscle wall of the womb. The catheter may then attach itself to pieces of bowel and, when it is withdrawn will pull after it through the womb and out into the vagina, a damaged and often torn piece of bowel. When this happens it is necessary to make an incision and open up the lower abdominal cavity, pull the bowel back through the hole in the womb, repair the womb and the bowel. Other less common causes of death after abortion are shock, kidney failure, clots, air embolism and complications of general anaesthesia.

Professor Sir John Stallworthy, of Oxford, one of the most distinguished of gynaecologists, published in the *Lancet* as long ago as December 1971 a critical assessment of the risks of abortion. He said: 'Unfortunately, because of emotional reactions to legal abortion, well-documented evidence from countries with a vast experience of it, received little attention in either the medical or the lay press. . . . The public is misled into believing that legal abortion is a trivial incident, even a lunch-hour procedure, which can be used as a mere extension of contraceptive practice. There has been almost a conspiracy of silence in declaring the risks. This is medically indefensible when patients suffer as a result'. In case anyone attempts to discredit Sir John as a middle-class Christian who is prejudiced against abortion and therefore exaggerates its dangers, I invite them to compare his words with the following quotation: 'According to our findings many women assume that, provided an abortion is carried out at a hospital, all possibility of complications is thereby eliminated. This misconception is due to the comparatively simple way women are admitted to the gynaecological wards and their short stay there. We have ascertained that the majority of women are well acquainted only with the comparatively rare complications of an operation for the termination of pregnancy, ie perforation and haemorrhage. They are quite inadequately informed about the most prevailing consequences, ie gynaecological inflammatory diseases, frequent complications during subsequent pregnancies and confinement, disordered function of the ovaries and so forth. Therefore it is necessary to take more active measures based on up-to-date scientific data to combat the idea so firmly held by the public, that an abortion performed in hospital conditions is a perfectly safe and harmless operation'.

Not the words of a middle-class Christian, but the summary to a paper by S.L. Pochanova of the Central Scientific Research Institute of Health Education of the Ministry of Health of the USSR. These are the words of a good Communist who has observed the complications of abortion for a longer period than any western country.

Non-Fatal Complications of Early Abortion

The complications of an abortion performed in the first three months are less dangerous than those from a late abortion, but they are by no means negligible. Both general and local anaesthetics are not without risk, pneumonia following aspiration of vomit has been mentioned as a cause of death, but it doesn't always kill; local anaesthetic can cause an allergic reaction with dizziness, twitching and collapse. The operation itself can cause serious bleeding, necessitating blood transfusion and intensive care. This in turn may lead to anaemia and lowered blood pressure. Embolism is a complication whereby a blood clot, a piece of fat tissue or air gets into the blood stream during an abortion and circulates throughout the body, eventually getting stuck in some vital area where it may cause serious trouble or death. Infection after an abortion is so common that most of the abortion chambers give all the patients anti-biotics in an effort to prevent the infection getting hold. In a series of 1,182 abortions reported in the *Lancet*, 312 women developed fevers of over 100°F. Infection in most cases is mild, but even mild infections can have serious after-effects. Perhaps the most tragic after-effect of post-abortion infection is where the infection spreads to the fallopian tubes. Sometimes it forms an abscess here, necessitating a further operation, but usually it clears up with antibiotics and the patients heaves a sigh of relief and says to herself 'Thank heavens that's all over, now I can forget it'. Many years later she may wonder why it is taking her so long to get pregnant. After a series of tests she will hear that the infection following her abortion caused her fallopian tubes to become completely blocked, and there is now no way that the egg from her ovary can pass down the tube to meet the sperm from her husband and make a baby. She is sterile.

I often wonder how many women on the waiting list for *in vitro* fertilisation are in this sad position because they had their first baby aborted. Sir John Peel, formerly the Queen's gynaecologist and past President of the Royal College of Obstetricians and Gynaecologists, described as 'not unrealistic' a rate of five to ten per cent sterility following abortion. He was giving evidence to the Select Committee of the House of Commons on Abortion in 1975. The *Daily Telegraph* of 23rd May 1980 reported that Mr. Robert Winston, a gynaecologist who runs an infertility clinic in London's Hammersmith Hospital, said one woman in three whom he saw with damaged fallopian tubes had had an abortion. He said he did not oppose abortion, but continued: 'The danger of abortion causing infertility should perhaps be pointed out before people get pregnant, so that they take more care over contraception'.

An ectopic pregnancy has already been mentioned; it is frequently associated with infection. Post-abortion infection is known to be the cause of a later ectopic pregnancy. In a normal conception the egg from the ovary meets the sperm from the husband in the fallopian tube. Where infection has caused sterility the tube is so blocked, the egg can't pass down to meet the sperm; where the damage to the tube is not so severe the egg is able to meet the sperm and the wife conceives. The embryo grows quickly, but because of adhesions and scarring from the infection, it can't squeeze through the obstruction in the tube and reach the safe harbour of the uterus. It is the nature of an embryo to implant itself and if it can't reach the uterus the embryo, so to speak, 'beds down' in the fallopian tube and starts to grow. The result is always disastrous for the mother and child. There has been a 300 per cent increase in ectopic pregnancies in the United States since abortion was legalised. In 1970 the incidence was 4.8 per 1000 live births, by 1980 it had risen to 14.5 per 1000 live births. One of the most serious gynaecological conditions has increased threefold since abortion became easily available.

'Retained Products of Conception' is a technical way of saying that a piece of the placenta or a piece of the baby has been left behind in the womb. It causes both bleeding and infection and makes another operation necessary, thereby doubling the risks. Perforation of the wall of the womb by the curette or Karmen catheter is not rare, nor is tearing the muscles at the neck of the womb. Perhaps the commonest complication of early abortion is due to the stretching of the neck of the womb at the start of an abortion. Unless this is done very carefully the muscle may tear (the pregnant womb is much softer than the non-pregnant one). If the tear is deep, there can be serious bleeding and the muscles must be stitched. This is not common, but smaller tears of muscle fibre are very common, particularly if the abortion is for a woman's first pregnancy. If a woman has had a baby the neck of the womb will already have stretched widely enough to allow a baby's head and body to pass through and be born. This opening of the muscles at the mouth of the womb before birth and their closure afterwards, shows how wonderfully the special muscles which form the womb are made. Where a woman is childless the neck of the womb is tightly closed and more liable to be damaged when violently forced open by dilators. The damage done is not realised by either the patient or her doctor until it is too late. The effect of the damage done to the cervical canal is discovered when the woman decides to have a baby. In a later pregnancy as many as one-third of those women who had an abortion for their first pregnancy will have a miscarriage or a premature labour. The reason for this is that the neck of the womb has lost its ability to close tightly and when the baby reaches a certain size the neck opens up. I have seen women with a baby's foot and leg hanging out through the cervical canal at twenty-two weeks of pregnancy, a condition due to this muscle damage which is called 'incompetent OS' (OS is the technical name for the opening at the vaginal end of the cervical canal). A survey done in a hospital in Bristol and reported in the *British Medical Journal* in 1976, showed that the women who had had a previous abortion had a 17.5 per cent miscarriage rate in subsequent pregnancies, compared with 7.5 per cent in women who had not had an abortion.

There can be no doubt (reports have been compiled world-wide) that an abortion causes tears, sometimes microscopic, in the cervical canal, and these are the cause of later miscarriage and premature delivery. A premature baby needs special care and is more likely to be handicapped than a baby born at full term. One of the common indications for abortion is that the baby may be born handicapped and many thousands of late abortions are performed in an affort to prevent the birth of a live handicapped child. It is ironic that at the same time as costly and unpleasant tests are done on pregnant women to see if they are carrying a handicapped child, the abortionists, by their damage to the cervix, are causing extra premature and possibly handicapped children to be born. Estimates suggest that our doctors are responsible for the birth of more handicapped children than they prevent by their tests and late abortions for possible Downs children or spina bifidas. In the six years following liberalisation of abortion laws in Japan, the birth rate decreased by thirty-one per cent but the number of handicapped infants who died increased by forty-three per cent.

Margaret and Arthur Wynn in 1972 did a world-wide

survey of the after-effects of abortion and showed that abortion *increases:*

Sterility;
Pelvic inflammatory conditions;
Premature birth by at least forty per cent;
Ectopic pregnancy 150 per cent;
Spontaneous miscarriage thirty to forty per cent;
Longer and more painful labour in subsequent
  pregnancies;
The risk of retained or adherent placenta.

Complications of Late Abortion

Salting-out or saline abortion is rarely done in Britain – not because it is such a brutal method of killing, but because of the danger to the mother. There are two main risks of saline abortion, over and above the risks of all abortions. Brain damage, which can be permanent, has been reported due to seepage of the deadly saline into the mother's blood stream. The other serious complication, called 'disseminated intravascular coagulation' is a calamitous condition when the blood-clotting mechanism becomes disturbed, and clots occur in different parts of the body.

Prostaglandin abortions are just as unpleasant as saline abortions, but the side effects, though numerous, are not quite so severe. They have an unpleasant effect on the stomach; about half the patients suffer from nausea and vomiting and about a third get diarrhoea. Both saline and prostaglandin put the patient into premature labour. The pain from prostaglandin labour is greater than the pain from a normal childbirth, because the effect of the drug is to increase the pressure inside the uterus to levels way beyond that of normal labour. Prostaglandin should never be given to a patient who has had a previous Caesarean section, because the force of the prostaglandin-induced contractions could cause the scar to tear and the patient would then suffer from the serious emergency of a ruptured uterus. Tears of the neck of the womb are common.

The third method of performing a late abortion, hysterotomy; is rarely used. The reasons are both social and medical. The patient will need to stay a minimum of five days in hospital after this 'mini-Caesar', and cost is important, whether it is borne by the state or the patient. A general anaesthetic lasting for around thirty minutes is necessary and brings its own risks. Haemorrhage and infection are not common, but do occur. Perhaps the main contra-indication to a hysterotomy is the permanent scar left in the womb of the patient. If the woman's family is completed, hospitals will combine the operation with sterilisation by tying the fallopian tubes. If her family is not completed, she immediately puts herself into the 'at-risk' category. She must be carefully watched throughout pregnancy and especially so during labour, in case the scar in the womb tears and she ruptures her uterus. Many doctors insist that any patient of theirs who has had a hysterotomy, may not deliver naturally but must be delivered by Caesarean section.

I have left the complications of the 'D and E' (dilatation and evacuation) abortion till last, because I find it repugnant even to write about it. One of the more revolting complications was discussed at a conference of Planned Parenthood doctors at Miami Beach in 1977. This complication occurred after all the baby had been torn to bits and all the pieces pulled out except the head, which, with its sharp spicules of bone left behind in the uterus created a critical complication. Damage to the cervical canal is much more common because in order to remove a baby of this size (12–20 weeks) the opening must be much greater. The wall of the uterus is stretched more and therefore thinner. This increases the risk of perforating the uterus. Retained products of conception can be left behind, and it is in an effort to prevent this, that the nurse is given the horrible job of collecting the torn bits

75

of baby and making sure none is missing. Patients prefer a 'D and E' to a prostaglandin abortion because they do not have to go through a labour which can be as lengthy as any normal childbirth. Doctors and nurses do not. Even hardened abortionists find it unpleasant to have to grab at the leg of a living, wriggling baby and tear it off. But money is a great healer of frayed sensitivities, and this method of abortion is used more on paying patients than on those in state hospitals.

Effects on the Mother's Mental Health

The patient who starts to bleed a few days after her abortion rarely goes back to the abortion chamber; she is usually admitted to her local hospital for treatment. The patient with blood clots or bronchopneumonia could not be treated by an abortionist in a place with no facilities for treatment of such conditions. It is some years before a woman discovers that she has been made sterile by her abortion. Abortionists are therefore able to claim that they see hardly any post-abortion complications. There is now, however, a considerable amount of literature from all over the western world, and also from behind the Iron Curtain, which proves beyond doubt the serious effect of abortion on the physical health of the mother, particularly during a later pregnancy.

From my own experience I believe that, though the physical after-effects can be both distressing and dangerous, the mental after-effects are worse. They not only affect a woman's relationship with her husband or lover, but they can be with her night and day for the rest of her life. Humanists deny that abortion affects a woman's mental health, and maintain that in the rare cases where depression occurs it is because the church and/or her Christian friends and family have, by their words and actions made her feel guilty. The expression I have heard used is: 'You certainly laid a load of guilt on that poor woman'. No one in the Pro-Life movement would ever attack the woman; but it is true that any woman who, believing it to be wrong, goes ahead and has her unborn child aborted will almost certainly suffer from guilt feelings. If she is a Christian she has the means to repent, seek God's forgiveness and be restored. But those who have no religion do not have this means of grace. Abortion is a sin against nature as well as against God. It is easy to scrape an unborn child from its mother's womb; it is very hard to scrape the memory of that child from her cerebral cortex. I had a friend who, like me, is a doctor. Many years ago she had an abortion, and a child at that time in her life would indeed have been very inconvenient (there is never any time in our lives when a newborn baby is 'convenient', that is why it is no good parents trying to play God). I didn't see her for many years and when I again met her she was divorced and remarried and had three healthy children. We celebrated our reunion with champagne. After about an hour of the typical 'Do you remember. . . . ?' sort of talk, she suddenly said 'Margaret, I killed my baby' – and burst into tears. I tried to comfort her and finally went to get her husband from the kitchen. I said to him 'I'm so sorry, it's my fault, seeing me again after all these years has reminded her of her abortion because I was around at the time, and of course she knows where I stand.' His reply amazed me – he said 'Don't blame yourself, it is nothing to do with you. There's never a month passes but she doesn't cry for that baby'. The significance of the story is that not only was this forty years after the abortion, but that my friend was an atheist and the child of atheist parents. She had never been in contact with religion, except briefly as a small child when she visited her grandparents.

It is not easy to discover how much mental distress and illness is associated with a previous abortion, and it is almost impossible to prove that it was the abortion that caused the illness, and not something else that may have occurred. There are, however, some facts which cannot be disputed and which point the finger quite clearly at the cause of the trouble. Death by suicide is always a tragedy, an attempted suicide is a clear sign that someone is suffering from a feeling of such hopelessness that life is no longer worth living. Evidence submitted to the Select Committee of the House of Commons on Abortion in 1975 by Dr Farmer and Miss Sally O'Brian from the Westminster Hospital, London, clearly showed a connection between abortion and attempted suicide. They had made a study of the attempted suicides admitted to their hospital over the years (one thousand each year were brought into the emergency room). In an effort to find out why so many, mainly young, people wanted to end their lives they looked into all the significant factors in their past and compared the results with a control group which consisted of the named best friend of each of the patients. The only significant factor to arise from the research was 'Of the overdose group twenty-nine per cent had abortions compared with thirteen per cent of the control group'. They conclude ' . . . the investigation suggests that either abortion and self-poisoning occur in the same type of individual, or that abortion increases the likelihood of self-poisoning'. So we can see that death can be the most serious mental after-effect of abortion, just as it is the most serious physical after-effect.

Between death by suicide and transient feelings of sadness there is a whole range of mental illness caused by abortion. Depression can be so severe as to interfere with the woman's ability to hold down her job. It can bring on physical side-effects. A patient of mine who became depressed after an abortion lost most of her hair. It is quite common for emotional disorders following abortion to reach a climax at the menopause – again, I have experience of menopausal women with depression who have told me that, though they have not told a soul till they unburdened to me, they have never got over the fact that they destroyed their own child. A World Health Organisation scientific group concluded: 'There is no doubt that the termination of pregnancy may precipitate a serious psychoneurotic or even psychotic reaction in a susceptible individual'. I would disagree with the last four words – when it comes to post-abortion depression, we are all 'susceptible individuals'. No one is immune. It is now accepted that there are no mental indications for abortion, abortion causes more mental illness than it could possibly cure. A lie that must be laid to rest is the pro-abortion claim that women who are unwillingly pregnant will commit suicide if they can't have a safe legal abortion. It could not be more wrong. Women are less likely to commit suicide when they are pregnant than at any other time in their lives. Statistically speaking, to reduce the suicide rate in women a foolproof method would be to keep every woman pregnant or breast-feeding from puberty to menopause!

These are two further mental after-effects which, while not serious of themselves, have disastrous side-effects. It is quite common for women to become frigid following an abortion, and cease to enjoy sex. This is easily understood; even those who support abortion on demand admit it is an unpleasant experience – it is only natural that sexual intercourse becomes associated with this unpleasant experience. Added to this may be a resentment against the father (who may have pressurised her to have the abortion), a feeling that it is utterly unjust that he should not have to endure any of the pain and trauma involved in the abortion when the pregnancy was indubitably a 'joint venture'.

The second complication is where the father of the child becomes impotent with the woman who had the abortion. This may be caused by the guilt he feels because he is at least partly responsible for what she has endured. Abortion falls on a relationship between man and woman as devastatingly as an early frost falls on a field of ripening wheat. The wheat and the relationship are both ruined. It is a fact that following an abortion, both sexual relationships outside marriage and marriages themselves break down – divorce, just like death, can be due to abortion.

As can be seen the consequences of abortion are many

79

and unpleasant, but it is important to point out again that the Christian has a more fundamental objection to it. Killing the defenceless child in the womb is wrong of itself and even if it had no unpleasant after-effects, even if it had good after-effects and made the woman more intelligent and improved her figure it would *still* be wrong.

Not that I wish to condemn the women; as victims they suffer enough, and I pray they may be able to find their peace with God. But I condemn totally – and I would like to shout my condemnation from the roof tops – those doctors who make a small fortune from killing the unborn and harming the mothers, and those journalists and television and radio producers who suppress the side-effects of abortion and pretend to be 'caring' because they support abortion for any woman who wants it. That is hypocrisy.

6

The War of Words

'Woe unto them that call evil good and good evil, that put darkness for light and light for darkness, that put bitter for sweet and sweet for bitter'. *Isaiah 5: 20 – 21*

'We're going to do a little test, Mrs. Jones, just to see if your baby's doing all right'.

How innocent that sounds! The test is an amniocentesis, or amnio test. It can't be undertaken early in pregnancy because it consists of passing a long needle through the mother's skin, fat, muscles, and wall of the womb into the baby's place of residence. A small amount of the fluid surrounding the baby is drawn off and this is tested. The object of this minor surgery is to ascertain the sex of the baby, and whether it has Downs syndrome, spina bifida, or other congenital defects. The reason it is important to know the sex of the unborn child is because certain hereditary diseases only affect boys (probably the best known of these is haemophilia – the bleeding disease). The fact that the child is a boy doesn't necessarily mean he will have inherited the disease, but if it is a girl, the parents know that, though she can carry the disease she will not suffer from it. Many parents, with the total agreement of their doctors, refuse to take the risk and therefore have all their sons killed off at about the fifth month of pregnancy. Likewise, if the test shows the child is suffering from a handicap it will be destroyed.

It is hard to imagine a more objectionable form of discrimination, and it is a fact that has never ceased to amaze me that some of the most liberal of doctors who oppose all forms of discrimination on the grounds of sex, race, colour or creed, aggressively support this most blatant form of discrimination, namely the killing of the handicapped. We are used to passing tests for various reasons – to be a soldier, to go to university, to be allowed to drive; today in our so-called civilised society, it is necessary for babies to pass a test to be allowed to be born alive. The first test is whether our parents want us, and the second whether we are perfect in every way. If we are handicapped, or if there is a possibility that we have a hereditary disease, we fail the test and may be killed before birth. Fortunately most Christians do not accept this form of discrimination and refuse to have the amnio test on the grounds that even if the child were shown to be handicapped they would refuse to have an abortion.

'Compassion' is a beautiful word. It means suffering with someone, sharing their burden of suffering, and relieving it if possible. This lovely word is constantly debased by abortionists, who maintain that their work is humanitarian, and that it is compassion which prompts them to kill the unborn, because they love them too much to let them be born when they are not wanted, or handicapped. Dr Donald De Marco, in his book *Abortion in Perspective* writes: 'Abortionists see themselves as purgers. Through abortion things are made better, life is purified. The death of the unborn improves its lot. Possible rejection or being born handicapped is, to these purifiers, a fate worse than death'. There's nothing new about this sort of rationalisation; Shakespeare described it well when he wrote of Brutus and Cassius attempting to convince themselves that they were acting humanely and even lovingly by killing Caesar. Dr De Marco quotes most aptly:

Why he that cuts off twenty years of life
Cuts off so many years of fearing death.
Grant that, and then death is a benefit.

So are we Caesar's friends, that have abridged
His time of fearing death.

He adds: 'The murder of Caesar promised to Brutus and
Cassius a future of peace and liberty. That day never came'.
The late abortion of the handicapped child casts its shadow
forward. Once it became accepted that it was good medical
practice to search for and destroy the imperfect child in the
womb, it was not long before our caring and compassionate
doctors took it upon themselves to destroy the born handicapped in the cradle.

Newspeak came before 1984

All revolutions in ethics are preceded by a revolution in
language. It is necessary that society have the impact
cushioned by a thick bed of euphemisms. Doctors who do
abortions avoid using the word; they say: 'We'll arrange a
termination'. It's not correct – if they used the expression
'premature termination of pregnancy' it would be more
accurate. *All* pregnancies are terminated, usually at about
nine months; it is totally false to muddle up termination of
pregnancy, which is normal, with extermination of the
unborn, which is not. Sometimes the even more ridiculous
phrase 'interruption of pregnancy' is used, as if the pregnancy
was going to continue after it had been 'interrupted'.

When any woman has a spontaneous miscarriage, no
matter how early in the pregnancy, the doctor will say 'I'm
sorry, Mrs. Brown, I'm afraid you've lost your baby'. But yet
the same doctor, ten minutes later will say to a woman who
wants an abortion, 'I'll arrange for a termination'. He does
not say 'I'll get rid of your baby for you' – if he mentions
the child at all he will call it a 'foetus'. Why on earth should
the child in the womb be called a baby when it's wanted,
and a foetus when it's not? Beware of people who use Latin
words when there's a perfectly good Anglo-Saxon one. They

usually use a Latin word because they don't really want you to know what's happening. Doctors are perfectly capable of explaining the facts of their patient's 'illness' in plain English if they want to. If they don't – watch out! They're trying to hide something. It is essential for the abortion industry that ordinary people do not know what is in the womb (I am positive that if we had clear plastic fronts to our wombs, there would hardly be any abortions performed). Some doctors will never use the expression 'unborn' or 'preborn' child, but always the word 'foetus' (which means 'the little one') because it doesn't sound at all human. Other words used for the unborn are 'gametic material', 'foetal marmalade', 'bits of jelly', 'mass of tissue'. We are all guilty of using euphemisms, we talk of death as 'passing away', we call false teeth 'dentures', and slums 'sub-standard housing'. We do it because we don't like facing up to a reality which may be unpleasant. Abortion counsellors use the word 'client' for an expectant mother – who is not 'pregnant', but only a 'woman with a problem' (which they of course will help to 'sort out'). Everything is done to dehumanise the unborn child. George Orwell, in his most prescient book *1984*, describes exactly why the language has to be changed: there is always a proletariat (abortionists are appallingly elitist) which must not be allowed to realise what is happening.

Pornography, not Truth

An interesting example of censorship is what happened to the video '*The Silent Scream*'. This is an utra-sound film of what actually happens during an abortion. It was made by Dr Bernard Nathanson. That fact alone is remarkable because he was a co-founder of the American pro-abortion organisation and performed over five thousand abortions himself. He is a man of no religion, though, significantly, he has a Jewish background. As a gynaecologist he became interested in the development of the unborn child, and from his studies he came to realise that it was impossible to deny that the child in the womb was a human being. From then on, he has become a great fighter in the pro-life battle. This has been at some considerable cost to himself. He is hated and repeatedly attacked by his former friends and colleagues, which is very hard to take. Without any religious faith behind him to support him, he had the courage to stand up and say: 'I was wrong'. He now gives up time and money to fight for the unborn, and in so doing he has set an example to many a Christian doctor.

The Silent Scream shows a twelve week baby peacefully sitting in its mother's womb, waving an arm occasionally and giving a kick every now and then. At one stage it is possible to see that its thumb has gone to its mouth. The heart is beating at a rate of 120 per minute. We then see the vacuum aspirator pushing through the cervix into the womb. Instantly everything changes – the heart beats much faster and the baby thrashes around wildly, backing away from the threatening nozzle of the aspirator. Finally we can see the baby dismembered and nothing is left but the head which is removed with a special pair of forceps. Dr Nathanson explains and demonstrates throughout, so that even those who have never seen an ultra-sound picture or an X-Ray can make out the pictures.

Dr Nathanson showed the video for the first time in the Grand Committee Room of the House of Commons in late 1984. It was seen by a large number of Members of the House of Commons and the House of Lords, as well as the Press. It was immediately attacked as being fraudulent. With one exception it was completely ignored by the television, who maintained they could not show it because it hadn't been proved to be genuine. The same branches of the media which insist on the right to show simulated copulation on the television screen and simulated sodomy on the stage because of their abhorrence of censorship, effectively censored *The Silent Scream*. In the US, possibly due to the

85

greater competition between television channels, it was shown in most areas, but in both countries it was attacked as a fake. We were told in Britain that the wild thrashing movements of the child were made artificially by moving the head of the ultra-sound. This is quite false, because moving this head gives a completely different picture to the one given of arms and legs thrashing wildly in all different directions. We were told that the child would not be moving at all because the general anaesthetic given to the mother, would put the child to sleep. This argument holds very little water in the United States, where most of their early abortions are performed under a local anaesthetic. It has little validity here, because for all anaesthetics the lowest dose possible is given for the sake of the mother's health, and only rarely would the child be anaesthetised. The constant argument of the pro-abortion lobby was: 'the foetus can't feel pain'. Yet there is no doubt that from six weeks at the latest the child in the womb can feel pain – were it a puppy in the womb of a bitch shown on the ultra-sound, no one would deny that its tearing to pieces would be a brutal act, but because it is a human child so horribly killed, enormous efforts are made to deny that pain is suffered by the child. But what about that heart rate? You cannot explain away the increase in the heart rate, which rises from 140 to 200 beats per minute. This proves beyond doubt that before its dismemberment the child is in a state of terror.

Sad to say, the clergy are almost as euphemistic in their language as politicians. The Archbishop of York, in a letter to *The Times* on 4th September 1985, wrote 'In practice most contentious ethical issues arise in the murky area where principles conflict, facts are ambiguous and differences are largely a question of degree' (The difference between those who believe in permissive abortion and those who don't, must be 180 degrees!) '. . . . there is a factual and interpretive element in the making of moral decisions which may well be ambiguous, even when the moral principles themselves are clear. It is thus possible to hold, as I do, that innocent human life is sacred and must not be destroyed, while at the same time admitting a degree of uncertainty about the ethical significance of the earliest and most fragile stages of embryonic development'. To be fair to the Archbishop he was speaking about research on human embryos, which he supported. He was answered by an Anglican clergyman Francis Gardom – 'Fragility is no monoply of the very young. The very old suffer from it too. If the "ethical significance" of an unborn child (especially with regard to its right to live) is related in any way to its fragility, there would seem to be no good reason for not applying this principle throughout life, particularly in the later stages, when further development in the favourable sense seems unlikely and the nuisance value greater.'

If you think the Reverend Francis Gardom was being harsh about the Archbishop, I would point out that the Archbishop's trumpet was blowing a very uncertain sound. On 3rd June 1985 in a letter to *The Times* he had written of the dangers of moral absolutism and stated 'There is no way of deciding on biological evidence alone, whether a newly fertilised human ovum is or is not a human person'. But with respect, Your Grace, what else can it be? And even if there is doubt as to whether the fertilised egg is human or not, it must be given the *benefit* of that doubt until proved otherwise. In the womb, from the moment this marvellous process of gestation takes place, a new life comes into being, that like all others is an infinite part of God's creation. If we cease to see it so, how can we hold to a religious faith that believes in the Incarnation?

The Archbishop is not the only Christian to give a less than clear lead. When I was on a pro-life lecture tour in Australia, I was told by a Roman Catholic priest that his assistant bishop had told the clergy of the diocese that they were not to preach on the subject of abortion because there might be somebody in the congregation who had had an

87

abortion and they might be made to feel guilty. (Isn't it odd nowadays the way guilt is something which 'progressive' clergy think should be banished from the face of the earth? I have always believed that guilt was a healthy thing in small doses – unless we can feel it now and then, we wouldn't bother to improve.) The bishop was on a sticky wicket, because someone in most congregations has probably committed adultery, another fornicated, another stolen something, another been proud and another lazy. If a priest may not preach on sin in case it upsets someone he might as well go up into the pulpit and read the telephone directory.

The Quality-of-Life Myth

A Methodist minister in Gloucestershire stood up after I had put the pro-life position at a meeting, and said 'You seem to be very concerned about the sanctity of life, don't you think you've got it wrong? It's the *quality* of life that counts, not the quantity'.

But what is meant by quality of life? Those who trot this argument out are vague about this, and if pressed will say – being wanted, being healthy, having enough money to be adequately fed and clothed and a good enough education to be able to fulfil our potential. Yet it is possible to have all these things but because of death, divorce or other family disabilities, to have a terrible life; it is also possible to have none of them and have a great 'quality of life'. Beethoven was the child of poor parents, his father had syphilis and drank too much and his sister was mentally backward. Oh boy! Just imagine if they'd had social workers and a free health service in those days, what enormous pressure would have been put upon Mrs. Beethoven to have an abortion. (Another wonderful escape by a musician was described by Artur Rubinstein the famous pianist. In the February 26th 1966 edition of *Time* magazine he is quoted as saying 'My mother didn't want a seventh child, so she decided to get rid of me before I was born. Then a marvellous thing happened, my aunt dissuaded her and so I was permitted to be born. Think of it! It was a miracle!' Audiences all over the world had reason to be grateful to that aunt!)

It is amazing that people should believe so much in the value of material possessions that they consider them *vital* for quality of life. A Dr J. Adlam, writing to *Medical News* on 6th April 1977, said: '. . . . I am not afraid to stick by my belief that only those couples who have the necessary material possessions and sources of income to ensure an economically secure and safe cradle, should *allow* (emphasis mine) a pregnancy to progess to term'. Even more surprising is a statement of evidence to the Select Committee on Abortion by Mrs. Margaret Bramall, a high official of the National Council for One-Parent Families: 'For many girls adoption is not a substitute for a termination. Adoption for a maternal girl or woman is often the cause of grief and anguish. . . . often the girls who choose termination are those who are so responsible and maternal that they do not want to bring up their child alone, but cannot face adoption'. Here we have someone who runs a council for one-parent families saying that a child will suffer so much in a one-parent family that the responsible maternal girls choose to have their babies killed! She says quite rightly that adoption can cause grief and anguish, but the grief is for the mother; the child may gain great joy and happiness from being reared by adoptive parents. It is significant that many workers for Pro-Life were adopted children. They are glad there was no easy abortion when they were in their mothers' womb, because in spite of Mrs. Margaret Bramall's words, they are glad to be alive.

What is a good quality of life? It certainly isn't wealth. I have just read the biography of John Paul Getty, the richest man in the world, and he and his family seem to have the worst quality of life of anyone I have ever heard of. It's not success. Marilyn Monroe was beautiful, rich, and at the top of her profession, but she took her own life before she was forty years old. The new eugenicists insist that no handicapped person can have a decent quality of life. They forget about Helen Keller, born deaf and blind. She was enabled by the feeling of touch to learn speech and writing. She wrote books and graduated '*cum laude*' from university, and by her work she improved the outlook for both the deaf and blind-deaf. No one would doubt that her quality of life was far better than that of Marilyn Monroe. I have a cousin who has Downs syndrome. He has written a book, an autobiography, called *The World of Nigel Hunt*. It's not a brilliant book, but he needed no help with the spelling or typing (there he's ahead of me, I may have a university degree but I can't type). What shines out from the book is the fact that he enjoys life enormously, particularly music, both classic and modern jazz. I have not the slightest doubt that his quality of life is much greater than that of John Paul Getty the multimillionaire. We express great concern about the contemporary evils of war, violence, starvation, poverty, unemployment and inflation, but the greatest evil we face today is that of not caring for our neighbour, an evil that is as prevalent now as when Jesus told the parable of the good Samaritan.

The Samaritan did not decide that the traveller who fell among thieves was in such a bad way he would have a poor quality of life in the future. He did not take a knife and cut his throat because he believed it was compassionate to kill him. He put the injured man on his own ass and cared for him. I wish I could tie a huge banner across the door of every abortion chamber in the country, with letters a foot high which read: 'The Unborn Child is Your Neighbour'. Mother Theresa of Calcutta has no doubts at all about who is her neighbour; she has said: 'The biggest disease today is not leprosy or tuberculosis, but rather the feeling of being unwanted, uncared for and deserted by everybody'. Quality of life is nothing to do with wealth, beauty or riches, it is everything to do with relationships. There is only one thing that is essential to human beings – to be related through care to others in his society, and through prayer to God.

The Neo-Fascism of Amniocentesis

Amnio-tests are done on women over thirty-five because it is well known that older mothers are more likely to have a baby with Downs syndrome. But the test is by no means harmless. Following amnio-centesis there is a much greater risk of a late miscarriage. There is also a small risk of damage to the child, due to the needle either going directly into the baby or causing a tear in the membranes. The test is not foolproof. In many cases a child is reported as normal but is born with Downs syndrome, and vice versa. One of the saddest stories I heard was of a woman who had longed for a child all her married life, but only became pregnant when she was nearly forty. Because of her age she had an amnio-test. When the result came back some weeks later (it takes weeks not days to get some of the results) she was told this longed-for child was a Downs baby. After much heart-searching she agreed to have an abortion. This was done, as are most late abortions, by causing a premature labour. When the baby was born the staff were horrified to find the child was quite normal. The feelings of the mother do not need describing. Because of the damage to mother and child and the disastrous results of a wrong diagnosis, fewer gynaecologists in Britain are doing amniocentesis tests, and ultra sound is now so well developed that it can be used to diagnose such conditions as spina bifida.

I find the whole ethos behind these tests obscene; society is saying that only the perfect have the right to be born. Such an appalling discrimination against the handicapped is the exact opposite of today's prevailing orthodoxy, which quite rightly punishes discrimination on the grounds of colour or sex. It is exactly the opposite of what we are taught by Christ.

It is important to remember that the General Assembly of

the United Nations on 20th November 1959, unanimously adopted the Declaration of the Rights of the Child. It included two important principles which are broken somewhere every second of every day by the same countries who signed it – they are:-

(1) The child by reason of his physical and mental immaturity needs special safeguards, including appropriate legal protection before as well as after birth.
(2) The handicapped child shall be given the special treatment, education and care required by his particular condition.

It is the duty of Christians to demand that these conditions are upheld, and to help in every way they can those families where one of the children is handicapped. To our shame we do not do enough to help in these cases. In her book *Abortion Law Reformed* Madeleine Simms, one of the leading workers in the campaign for abortion on demand, wrote 'An abnormal foetus is not aborted because it would die if it were born, but on the contrary because it would be healthy enough to live a sub-human existence. Essentially it is for social, ethical and aesthetic (!) reasons that some people, including those on the Church of England and British Medical Association abortion committees, recoil from the survival of such subhumans and prefer to see them aborted.' This is pure fascism. One of Hitler's doctors wrote that society had a duty to forbid 'unsuccessful life' because society had to pay for it. A Nobel prizewinner, Sir Peter Medawar, at one time Head of the Medical Research Council, was quoted in the House of Commons by Renée Short, MP, as saying: 'No one has conferred upon parents the right to produce maimed or biochemically crippled children'.

The handicapped child in the womb has a universally bad press. Few voices speak up for him and those that do are not reported in the press or heard on TV or radio. And so, little by little, western society slipped yet further down the slippery slope. It is a fact of physics that anything going down a slope gathers speed, and the further the faster. Starting with reluctantly permitting abortion for the 'overburdened mother', the principle of killing expanded, as all principles do, to its utmost limits, and a few years ago it became obvious that doctors were killing newborn babies who were handicapped. Infanticide, the morally unthinkable of one generation, became accepted in the next.

From Foeticide to Infanticide

I believe the threat of infanticide has been there ever since abortion became both legally and socially acceptable in the west. When abortion was illegal except for genuine medical reasons, and socially abhorrent, no one dreamed of killing a baby. Today the argument is simple and even rational; it goes like this: 'If you can kill a perfectly healthy normal baby of twenty-four to twenty-eight weeks by abortion because it is unwanted, why should you want to protect a defective child at birth?' Joseph Fletcher, in an article published in 1978, called 'Infanticide and the Ethics of Loving Concern', wrote: 'It is reasonable to describe infanticide as post-natal abortion'. (Dr Fletcher is, of course a major proponent and populiser of situation ethics, a system which denies the existence of absolute values.)

Forty years after the end of World War II we are emulating the activities of the Nazis. The parallels in the progress downhill are alarming. Just as German children had eugenics drawn into questions of mathematics, so anti-life propaganda today is directed against the young in this country. In January 1978 the French A-Level paper set by the University of London included the question: 'In our times society attaches too much importance to protecting and sustaining the poor, the handicapped and the old. What is your opinion? Develop your ideas.' In 1972 a Yale University geneticist, Dr Y.

Edward Hsia, speaking at a meeting of the American Association for the Advancement of Science, suggested compulsory
pre-natal tests to discover handicapped unborn babies, and
compulsory abortion if they were positive. In 1974 Dr Robert
Cooke, Vice-Chancellor of Medicine at the University of
Wisconsin, testified before the Senate Health Committee
that two thousand newborn babies die each year in America
because treatment is withheld. According to a report in the
Canadian Medical Association's journal in 1977, twenty-
seven children born with Downs syndrome have been allowed
to die in the Sick Children's Hospital in Toronto in the last
twenty years. The expressions 'allowed to die' and 'withheld
treatment' are euphemisms. No one needs permission to die,
doctors spend their lives trying to *stop* people dying. What it
really means is 'not allowed to live'. Other euphemisms used
when doctors murder newborn handicapped babies are –
'letting nature take its course', 'letting the baby slip away'.
They all sound so harmless and peaceful. In fact they are
harmful, cruel and violent.

There are various methods for killing babies and the
method depends on the type of handicap. There was a time
when nothing could be done for children with spina bifida
(a condition where the back has not joined completely,
usually at the bottom; a bit of bone is missing and the skin
over the base of the spine is absent). Most of these children
died at a few months old, but not all; some lived, but were
always paralysed in their legs to some extent. About twenty
years ago paediatric surgeons started operating on these
babies as soon as they were born. After this very few died, but
some were still left with paralysed legs, some were mentally
handicapped and sometimes an operation was needed to
stop water on the brain developing. After about ten years of
operating on all children, surgeons stopped and only operated
on those cases where they hoped that severe paralysis could
be prevented. But what about the others? That's the problem.
Certain hospitals did not let them go home, as they might

ethically have done, because their loving mothers might have cared so well for them that the skin healed up and the child survived. It was (and for all I know may still be) the practice to see that such disastrously crippled children did not leave hospital unless it was in a coffin. The usual method was to dope them with a sedative and feed them only water. Sometimes they doped them strongly and gave orders that they were to be fed 'on demand'.

The other large group of murdered children were Downs children born with an obstruction in the gullet. This can be treated by an operation which is not difficult and nearly always successful. It is performed at once on any normal baby because the child can receive neither milk nor water unless the gullet (oesophagus) is repaired. In the case of a Downs child, however, it is not done at once – the parents are told that their child will never be mentally normal, then asked if they want this operation performed; or would they prefer to 'let nature take its course?'. It is hard to imagine a worse time to be confronted with a life-and-death decision than shortly after you have delivered a child – just as a woman is unfit to decide on an abortion in the first three months of pregnancy. Were the child normal the mother would not be asked to decide, she would be told the child must have an operation at once and asked to sign a permission form. Where the mother is exhausted after, perhaps, a prolonged labour, and very upset that the child is not normal, it is hardly surprising that she will say, when prompted by the doctor – 'Perhaps we'd better let nature take its course'. After that the child is forced to suffer one of the most cruel deaths imaginable. Not a drop of liquid can pass into its stomach. The doctors, of course, dope these children heavily, otherwise their screams of hunger would upset the nurses and patients. And all this is implicitly approved by Nobel prizewinner Dr Crick, who was quoted by the Pacific News Service as follows: 'No newborn infant should be declared human until he has passed certain tests

95

regarding its genetic endowment and that if it fails these tests, it forfeits the right to live'.

A story is told of a biologist who did some research with frogs. He kept two frogs in a beautiful big tank with everything in it to make a frog happy. It also had a slope leading up to the top of the tank, so that at any stage the frogs could, if they wished, jump out of the tank. Then very slowly, by half a degree a day, the biologist heated the water in the tank. They were so happy with their playthings, and it all happened so slowly, that the frogs didn't notice that the water was heating up. Not in fact until just before they were boiled alive. The new ethic which judges each life by its supposed 'quality' is slowly – very slowly – taking over from the old ethic which believed that life was a gift of God, and, being given by Him, should only be taken by Him.

In Indiana the so-called 'Bloomington Baby' was a little Downs child with a gullet obstruction. The parents refused to allow treatment, refused to accept any of the many offers to adopt the child and won a court case to permit them to starve their child. A similar case in Britain had a happy ending. A Downs syndrome girl whom the press called Alexandria (not her real name) was born in a hospital in West London with an obstructed gullet. Again, her parents refused permission for her to have an operation. A brave doctor (it's usually nurses who are courageous in these cases, but this time it was a doctor) reported the case to the Director of Social Services. He went to court and got an order to put the child in the care of the Social Services. He then had some difficulty finding a hospital to do the operation, but eventually it was done and the child recovered well and went to a foster home. There is an interesting epilogue to this story – after some years the parents applied to the courts for custody of Alexandria, and to the distress of the foster mother her natural parents were given custody of the child they had wished to see dead.

Martin Luther King wrote: 'Morality cannot be legislated

for, but behaviour can be regulated. Judicial decrees may not change the heart but they can restrict the heartless.' The law in America was altered in May 1982, when the government, through the Health and Human Services Secretary, Richard Schweiker, warned 6,800 hospitals across the nation that they could lose government funds if they denied care to babies with birth defects or other handicap.

Perhaps the most famous case of the death of a Downs child in this country was that of John Pearson. He had no obstruction in his gullet and appeared to be very healthy at birth. He had a high birth rating, an APGAR score of nine out of ten. Downs children are characteristically mentally slow, but they are also cheerful, lovable, affectionate and good-natured. They are fond of music. John Pearson was one of the patients of Dr Leonard Arthur, a children's doctor. The mother was upset when told she had a Downs child, a few hours after the birth, and cried out that she didn't want him. Dr Arthur wrote on John Pearson's treatment sheet: 'Mother rejects. Nursing care only'. He was deprived of all food and given only water, with the addition of a very powerful drug similar to morphine, that had not been passed as safe to give to small children under four years old. John Pearson who suffered from no disease but was handicapped, died after three days of starvation, sedation and interference with his breathing by the drug. A brave nurse reported the case to the police, who were able to get hold of the body before it was cremated. The Crown pathologist said that death was due to an overdose of the drug DF 118, and that the body of the three-day old child contained more than the adult fatal dose. Dr Arthur was brought to trial, but as in the case of Dr Waddell of California, he was found not guilty. Obviously the members of the jury agreed with Peter Singer of the Centre for Bio-Ethics, Monash University in Australia, who wrote in a paediatric journal on 1st July 1983: 'If we compare a severely defective human infant with a non-human animal, say a dog or a pig, we will often find the non-

97

human to have superior capacities, both actual and potential, for rationality. Only the fact that the defective infant is a member of the species *Homo Sapiens* leads it to be treated differently from the dog or pig. Species membership alone is not morally relevant. . . . If we can put aside the obsolete and erroneous notion of the sanctity of all human life, we may start to look at human life as it really is, at the quality of life that each human being has or can achieve.'

Dr Arthur died a few years later of a brain tumour. When I heard it I wondered what John Pearson would say to him when they meet.

Be Fruitful and Multiply

'All things were made by Him and without Him was not anything made that was made.' *John 1: 3*

It has become fashionable to blame population growth for practically every evil that exists, national or international. In *Reader's Digest* December 1969 was an article called 'Standing room only on spaceship Earth', by a senior American legislator. It included the following: 'The numbers of people jammed into our large cities are increasingly ominous. Crime rates soar. . . . there is poverty, racial strife, the rotting of our central cities, the formless and ugly sprawl of urbanisation.' Mother Theresa, who really does know about crowded cities, said: 'More and more countries are afraid of the child, more afraid of babies than they are of bombs and guns.'

Panic about over-population is widespread, ridiculous claims are made which have no foundation in fact. 'Standing room only on spaceship Earth' is an example of hyper-exaggeration. In fact, the entire population of the earth could stand (if only stand) on the Isle of Wight. It might sink under the strain, but it's a very different picture from the one which we constantly get from our newspapers, that Britain is so grossly over-crowded that in another few years we shall tumble off the white cliffs of Dover.

Many years ago Malcolm Muggeridge put the facts succinctly when he said: 'Britain has a copulation explosion, not a population explosion'.

In fact for the developed world the problem is not a population explosion, but a population 'implosion'. With very few exceptions the white races of the world are not reproducing themselves, families are getting smaller and smaller, and as the birth rate goes down the divorce rate goes up. With the re-marriage of their parents, perhaps even twice, children find themselves with an assortment of step-mothers and step-fathers. We shall soon have a situation where, instead of asking parents 'How many children do you have?', we shall be asking children 'How many parents do you have?' I do not know whether having only two children leads to their happiness, but I have no doubts that having only two parents does!

I believe the population explosion to be false, it is a fact that in some areas populations are increasing and in others decreasing, but the gloomy forecasts that we hear so much today are about as valid as the gloomy forecasts of the 'Yellow Peril' were in our grandfathers' time. There are many estimates of the size and rate of growth of the world's population, but very few hard facts. 'Estimates', even when put out by impeccable sources, are only 'guesstimates'. My brother once asked President Tubman of Liberia, what was the population of his country – he replied that, alas, he had been unable to find out because their attempts at a census of population were always unsuccessful. When pressed to elaborate, he said: 'The first time we tried, the people in the villages thought it might be something to do with taxes, so they hid as many of the villagers as they could and the result we got was absurdly low. Realising what was happening, we tried again after dropping hints that we might be considering a children's allowance. The villagers, not being stupid, produced all their own children and borrowed children from other villages, so we got a result this time that was ridiculously high – we presume the figure is somewhere between the two, but we can't be sure.'

Population experts realise that many of the poorer nations do not have accurate figures for their populations. As long ago as 1974, figures appeared in *Population and Family-Plan-*

ning Programs: a Factbook, that showed that of the thirty-one countries usually listed as highly developed twenty-one had birthrates below replacement levels. At that stage in the United States, the population had declined fifty per cent in sixteen years. The enormous propaganda efforts in the United States to reduce their population are strange in view of the huge amount of empty space they have. There are only twenty-two people per square kilometre there, compared with between one hundred and three hundred in different parts of Europe. To most people's surprise Holland is the most densely populated country in the world, but that country is by no means the poorest, rather is it one of the most stable and prosperous. Two academic economists, Herman Kahn and Julian Simon, have pointed out a fact that ought to be obvious, that prosperity has little to do with population density or even the presence of natural resources. From the following figures it is possible to see that there is no connection at all:-

Population Density per Square Mile

Bangladesh	1,530	India	572	West Germany	642
Mainland China	842	Japan	810		
Hong Kong	12,926	United States	64		

At this stage more people will be saying – 'It's not the amount of space available but the quality of the space, you can't grow corn on the top of the Rocky Mountains.' This is quite true, but an enormous amount of the earth's surface is wasted – a major survey of world food resources published by the University of California in 1974 showed that the world then was only using half the available arable land. Therefore without even any improvement in agricultural methods, the world could feed twice its present population. The continents differ in their use of land, Africa uses less than a third of its available arable land, whereas Asia uses three-quarters.

The European Death-Wish

I don't know who said: 'Whom the gods wish to destroy they first make mad', but the social statistics for Europe would seem to endorse it. The amount of food produced in Europe is so great that it is a cause of acute embarrassment, and even violence as French farmers try .to stop Italian lorries importing wine and fruit into France. But while the earth brings forth its cornucopia, in the developed nations the human inhabitants have reduced their fertility to below replacement level.

According to René Bel in *Children are our Future:* 'The century 1870 – 1970 saw a change in the demography of Europe, the major medical progress made in the nineteenth century meant that life expectancy increased. Contrary to the picture usually presented of the Victorian paterfamilias with his brood of twelve children, the number of children per family fell during the last third of the nineteenth and the first third of the twentieth centuries. World War II altered this and after the war there was an upturn in the birthrate which lasted into the sixties. In 1965, in all countries of Europe a rapid decline set in and the birthrate fell a phenomenal thirty to fifty per cent.

'This phenomenon is not confined to Europe but applies to all the "developed" countries, irrespective of the politics of their governments. By 1980 only Ireland (North and South) had an average of three children per family, all the rest, Europe (East and West), the USSR, Japan and Australia, had under 2.5 children per family, which allows for only very slight growth. But even more remarkable, Poland, Rumania and the USSR (despite of its fertile Muslim Asian republics) were producing below the survival level of 2.1 children per family.'

The reason for this is obscure. It is not due to the increased efficiency of contraception or the availability of abortion, because Europe had, in the thirties, produced a situation of zero population growth. One interesting aspect of this fact is that in the thirties there was a world-wide slump, poverty was desperate even in a comparatively wealthy Europe. In the sixties Europe and the rest of the developed world was enjoying an unprecedented boom. In Britain we were told by our government: 'You've never had it so good'. Materially speaking they were right, but in most other ways they were wrong. Divorce has never been higher (only in Ireland, Italy and Greece is it below 1 per 1000 population), and in 1981 demographic statistics showed only Ireland, Greece, Luxemburg and Belgium with no abortions. Denmark aborted 42.9 of every 100 babies conceived; Italy aborted just over one in three; France and Britain about one in five; West Germany and Holland slightly less. In spite of Denmark killing more children in the womb than any other country, just over one in three of their babies are born illegitimate, which shows how little there is to the argument that easily-available abortion reduces illegitimacy.

As I sat down this morning to write this chapter I received through the post the Draper Fund Report for September 1985 (The Draper Fund is a major supporter of population countdown proposals). It contained an article on Africa, where for many reasons there is, in some areas, poverty and hunger. Written from West Africa, it includes the following: 'Yet the solutions to the problems of over-rapid population growth cannot be imposed from outside or from the top down. They must be part of the framework of the African woman's way of life and thinking. African village women do not perceive themselves as unloved, sad or poor. They are quick to smile, sing, dance and embrace their children. When asked what they like most they reply: "To cook, to take care of my children and to be happy with other women". If asked what makes them unhappy they tell us – "To see my children get sick and die." ' I have no doubt at all that these simple women are not only happier but nearer to God's heart than the rich, well-fed European women with their high rates of divorce, abortion and illegitimate children.

Here in Europe our continent is becoming a land of old people, we are entering a situation which is called 'the inverted triangle'. Instead of few old but many young people, we now have few young and many old. The consequences of this situation are serious. A fall in the birthrate increases the unemployment rate. This is perfectly obvious, the old do not buy a lot of things, the young are the great consumers of everything from fizzy drinks to the latest fashion in clothes. Without babies we do not need toy factories or cradle-makers, without schoolchildren we do not need teachers or school books. The list is endless, yet I have heard it said that if we could halve our population we could do away with unemployment. The halving would have to start with the over sixty-fives, not the babies; without this, the problem caused socially by a large elderly population would over-whelm the social security system.

There are considerable problems even today with our large numbers of pensioners and small numbers of people to look after them. Medical science has succeeded in raising the expectation of life in the west to over seventy, but society does not want to provide adequate finance for their care. In the past the grandparents would have had enough children living near enough to help them in their old age. Now, with people moving away from their home towns more than previously, and families getting smaller and smaller, the State needs to put more and more of the taxpayers' money into the care of the elderly.

There have been two unpleasant side-effects of this system. In the past, with few exceptions, old age had not been considered something to be jeered at. Today it is common to find the elderly the butt of jokes in the media; but more sinister than that, there is an increasingly loudly-heard demand for euthanasia. We are assured that this will be voluntary and something which must be arranged by the subject at least three months previously, and only available when two doctors certify the patient to be suffering from an incurable disease. Personally, I put very little trust in two doctors certifying the presence of an incurable disease, because the Abortion Bill laid down that 'two doctors must certify in good faith that the risk to the mother's health of the pregnancy continuing, is greater that if the patient were aborted.' We know that has led to abortion on demand, without the second certifying doctor even seeing the patient. Why should it be any greater a safeguard in euthanasia? After all, we have seen already that the elderly persons life is no easier to justify than that of the crippled foetus. In recent judicial sentences, where wives have killed their husbands or husbands have killed their wives, all that is necessary is a good lawyer who will make out that because the spouse was senile, chronically sick or suffered pain, the husband acted out of 'compassion' to put her out of her misery.

Why did the population of the developed world slump at a time of prosperity? The answer lies in the decency of the ordinary people and the power of the media. Ever since the late sixties, press and broadcasting have spread panic about the exploding population; we have been told it is selfish to have more than two children, because to do so would mean another child in a poor part of the world going short of food. This strikes a very hollow note today, when Europeans are wasting money that could be used to help the underdeveloped world by using it to build ever bigger 'barns' to store wheat, butter and other food surplusses. This same panic about overpopulation was very useful to those who helped to steer through the Abortion Act in 1967. Even highly intelligent people believed the propaganda. I remember a teacher bringing two lovely boys of two and five years old to a baby clinic. She told me she would love to have a girl. When I asked her why she didn't have another child which might be a girl, she replied that she was a Christian and it would be wrong for her to have another child when babies were starving in India. Families have been bombarded with pessimistic forecasts of all kinds, from the destruction of the whole world by hydrogen bombs to a new Ice Age, which have added to the baby famine. Parents have understandably reacted against bringing children into such a dreadful world.

What caused the 'Population Growth'?

There is no doubt that in the underdeveloped countries there is a great increase in births, and the majority of the population is young. The reason is the increase in the efficiency of antibiotics, vaccines and antiseptics, together with an increased knowledge of hygiene and nutrition. Despite a definite rise in gross national production in most third world countries, poverty has often increased owing to famine, or civil and foreign wars, during which the money that should have gone to feed the hungry has gone to buy guns.

But the poor countries of the world might have been in a better state had western aid concentrated more on support for baby clinics, and less on contraception and abortion facilities. Aid for population control has gone up much faster than aid for health and agriculture, on the principle that if they have fewer children the health of both children and parents will improve automatically. In fact they have got it the wrong way round; if the health of the children improves, the parents will not have to worry about a childless old age. This is the nightmare of peasants in all the underdeveloped world. Women must have sons in Asia, because traditionally when the daughter marries she becomes part of the mother-in-law's household and cannot return to care for her own mother. In certain religions, a man believes that if his son is not there to close his eyes after his death, he will not be able

to enter Nirvana. In view of the fact that so many children die before they grow up, it would be a feckless man who didn't try for at least two sons and preferably three. The reason that poor peasants have child after child is because they need the children to help till the fields, and as they grow old they need their sons to provide food for them, otherwise they would starve. If half the money that had been spent trying to persuade or coerce Asian and African peasants to have fewer children had been spent on old age pensions, the problem would have been solved. With the fear of a hungry old age removed, people would regulate their families themselves.

Faced with the apparent refusal of third world couples to limit their families voluntarily, the western powers, and principally the United States, have struggled to find compulsory limitations which don't actually look as though they are compulsory. On 24th April 1977, the *St. Louis Post-Dispatch* (USA) reported that Dr Ravenholt, in charge of population problems in the American State Department at that time, had been unable to achieve his wish of making 100 million third world women incapable of bearing children. He was by no means alone in his wish – in a special supplement to Family Planning Perspectives (Planned Parenthood – World Population New York) dated 11th March 1969 Frederic Jaffe, who was at that time Vice-President of Planned Parenthood, suggested the following methods:

– Legalised abortion throughout the world;
– The possibility of introducing contraceptive substances into the drinking water, or basic commodity such as salt;
– Compulsory sterilisation for certain sections of the population;
– Compulsory pregnancy permits before starting a baby;
– Measures to encourage mothers to take jobs, and have small families;

– Encouragement of free childless unions among the young.

With the exception of doctoring the water supply with a contraceptive agent all of these methods have already been used somewhere. The encouragement of women to take jobs and thus have smaller families is probably one of the most powerful population control methods in the west. We are constantly bombarded with propaganda about how important it is for women to become managers, directors, judges and even bishops. A little thought will show that it's impossible to care properly for even a small family and give adequate time to succeed in such time-consuming jobs. Aspiring career women are the group of women most in favour of abortion on demand because the exigencies of climbing up the ladder of success exclude the possibility of a pregnancy. Successful career women, on the other hand, are not nearly so keen on abortion, because they realise what they have missed out on in their efforts to succeed. Quite often a woman will keep putting off starting a family until it is too late, and there is nothing she can do to bring back her fertility.

Because population countdown policies have been too successful in Europe, the European Parliament is having to consider methods to encourage fertility by extra family allowances, maternity and housing grants, an income for a mother who stays home to look after her children, flexitime and part-time jobs. These methods to encourage women to be good mothers are obviously sound common sense, for children are every nation's future. It has been estimated that unless the women in Sweden have a higher birth rate soon, there will be no more Swedes after four generations. It is easy to change laws and give extra benefits for mothers with children; what is not at all easy is to change attitudes, and unless that is done the population of the west will continue to decline. For twenty years we have been told by press, screen and radio that we should not have large families, everything has been geared to an anti-natalist policy. We are told that children are pollution. The attitude of international family planners to babies was typified by a headline in a family-planning magazine, about a new form of oral contraception which meant chewing small squares of impregnated paper. The headline read: 'Paper pills help to stamp out pregnancy'. Stamping-out is what you do to a cockroach.

What About Starvation in the Third World?

Our first concern must be about food. We are told most clearly by Our Lord to feed the hungry and that we must do before anything else. It isn't always easy, especially when we hear of stores of grain, meant to be feeding the hungry, lying on the dockside and being eaten by rats. Distribution and inequality pose real problems, but overall the picture is encouraging. According to *The Zero People*, edited by J. L. Hensley, 'Between 1962 and 1972 world food production increased thirty-one per cent, while world population increased twenty-one per cent. Rice production in Asia increased forty per cent during the nineteen-sixties, while population in Asia increased only twenty-five per cent. Wheat production has recently doubled in India which, though there is poverty and hunger in the country, is able to export food'. The book reports that Colin Clark, former Director of the Agricultural Economic Institute at Oxford University, and specialist on population resource questions, found that if all farmers were to use the best methods now in use, enough food could be raised to provide a western type diet for 35,100 million, nearly ten times the present population of the world.

Man does not live by bread alone; he also needs houses, clothes, television, radio and transport. We are repeatedly being told by environmentalists that the resources of the earth are finite. We are particularly warned of the imminent exhaustion of all energy sources and basic metals. But this isn't strictly true. Professor Julian Simon, of the University of Illinois, was the first person to show up the doomwatch myth in its true light. In articles in journals and several books, he has demolished the arguments of the 'doomwatchers' and shown that dire warnings that the planet Earth is running out of resources are nonsense. He has done careful calculations of the cost and availability of all of life's necessities from food and fuel to minerals, and he maintains that in fact nothing is ever actually 'used up', though it can be changed. It is possible to obtain usable metals from rubbish dumps, and it may be cheaper to re-cycle them than to obtain them from the ore. Perhaps more important is the use of substitutes. Copper is a valuable mineral in relatively short supply, but by using aluminium and steel to cook by, a great saving was made, and by putting a communications satellite into space, millions of miles of copper telephone wire were saved. Substitutes are sometimes of more use than the originals. At the beginning of this century, it became hard to get ivory to make billiard balls. A competition was held with a prize for whoever produced a substance as good as ivory for making billiard balls. It was won by a man who had developed a type of celluloid – the forerunner of plastics. In the sixteenth century the English were worried about the shortage of firewood, so they found coal. In the last century they believed that coal was running out so they turned to oil. Now we export both oil and coal!

But, it can be logically argued, in the end, no matter how many new coal- and oil-fields we find, coal and oil will run out. That must be true, but Professor Simon maintains that just as with ivory for billiard balls, a substitute will be found. Oil can come from coal, from rocks, from sand and also from plants such as rape and soya beans. In Brazil they are using alcohol with petrol to run their cars, and the use of alcohol as a form of fuel is being considered as one way of dealing with the glut of wine in Europe. Relatively recently our scientists have woken up to a fact they always knew, that all energy comes from the sun – at last throughout the hot countries and even dotted about in the temperate zones, are solar heat panels which collect the heat of the sun and use it to heat water. Before long it will be developed for cooking, and the power of the tides is already being harnessed to make electricity. Neither the sun nor the sea are finite resources.

The Dark Aspect of Population Control

Robert McNamara, while serving as Executive Director of the World Bank, is reported as saying about the problem of over-population, that if voluntary controls failed, nations would be driven to more coercive methods. Strangely, this philosophy is accepted by many of those who support abortion on demand, 'the woman's right to choose', in spite of the fact that the right to choose only works one way, the woman subject to population control has the right to get rid of her baby, but not to bring it into the world. The 'right to privacy' that was the reason given for the American Supreme Court's decision to allow abortion up to the ninth month of pregnancy is apparently not available for the poor of the third world, and those who scream for confidentiality in this country and 'privacy' in America are totally silent about the lack of it among their poorer sisters.

According to the World Bank (which is US based), in Indonesia they have village meetings which begin with a roll-call, each man responds by saying whether he and his wife are using contraceptives. Replies are plotted on a prominently displayed village map. In certain cases villagers who volunteer to have an intra-uterine device inserted will not only get extra food for themselves but for the whole village. Conversely, those who refuse will deprive their neighbours as well as themselves.

Bribery is a common method of persuading women either to be permanently sterilised (by having their fallopian tubes tied off) or temporarily (by the insertion of an intra-uterine device or an injection of a long-acting hormone contracep-

111

tive). An article in the *Lancet* June 30th 1984, written from Bangladesh, complained about the amount of money spent on so-called 'incentives', and saying that the resultant bias towards population control 'means that concern about health care, particularly for children, women and the rural poor, has been relegated mainly to the sphere of rhetoric'. What is ridiculous is that if these aid programmes spent more on child health, the over-population problem would go away. If their children are healthy enough to survive to adulthood, the women will control their own fertility without any 'incentives'. Population experts are angry that propaganda has not persuaded the deprived and landless peasants to contracept. (As Malcolm Muggeridge said: 'They asked for bread and you gave them multi-coloured condoms'.)

The article continues: 'The next step has been to get much tougher both with the government and with those on the direct receiving end, for their refusal to understand what is good for them'. Various ways of encouraging control were suggested to the government by a document supposedly originating from US Aid. These include all senior government employees being 'encouraged' to have a vasectomy (and guess what happens to their promotion prospects if they refuse), loss of salary increment for having a third child and a permanent ten per cent drop in pension for each individual child. Not surprisingly the government refused to accept these suggestions. The article continues to describe the efforts to make sterilisation acceptable in the villages: 'Each village is meant to be given a target for sterilisation procedures, and committees failing to meet this goal will, after a suitable warning period, simply find themselves going without any Aid funds that are around for projects such as tube wells or schools. Each village health worker has been given a specific number of women and men to be brought for sterilisation each month. The health worker is paid 2lbs. of rice for each person operated on. If a health worker fails to meet the target for six months, reduction in salary or dismissal will follow'.

The man or woman who is sterilised gets the equivalent of £6 and a deep blue sari.

This sounds more like coercion than bribery, and the impression is not reduced by a further sentence: 'Abuses of the system do happen, the range runs from simple inflation of figures to the rare excess (and one soon suppressed) of soldiers rounding up volunteers'. The writer of the article is particularly disturbed because incentives of all kinds, now account in Bangladesh for twenty per cent of US Aid's funds committed in this field. He adds: 'In Bangladesh child mortality remains cruelly high, and continuing neglect of this fact makes little sense, particularly since the fewer of her children who die, the greater the likelihood that a woman will use effective family planning ... The poor are already doing all they can to improve their precarious lives. Why should they always have imposed on them what others think they ought to want? Coercion in whatever form is, after all, an unpleasant and degrading way of coming to terms with fertility'.

So much for Bangladesh. The story of forced male sterilisation in India is well known and needs no repeating. It included such appalling facts as representatives of the government stopping buses at random and forcibly sterilising every male aboard, even if young and still childless (a much greater hardship in India than in Europe). There is increasing controversy in America over the use of 'incentives' in the underdeveloped countries, there is growing use of these 'incentives' in countries who receive US Aid and money from the United Nations Fund for Population Activities (UNFPA). The idea that the hungry poor should sacrifice their fertility for money or food is uncomfortably reminiscent of Jacob selling his birthright for a 'mess of potage'.

The most extreme example of compulsory fertility limitation is, of course, China. Before the present law which permits couples to have only one child each, various methods had been tried in efforts to reduce the population. The legal age for marriage had been raised, and the family allowance for a single child was lost when a second was born. These efforts did not produce a satisfactory response and the present draconian measures were imposed. It is particularly cruel on the Chinese because they have a special love of children and feel that each child brings more happiness into the home. Also there is no pension scheme in China; the old are supported by their children, who consider the work an honour. Under the new rules there are family-planning officers in each area who completely control the women of that area. Couples must marry late and are not allowed to have a child until they are given a red 'birth permission' card. These are allocated on a quota system to each commune or factory. After the birth of their only child, couples who sign a pledge to have no further children are given a special certificate which entitles them to free medical and nursery care. Factories and communes have family-planning workers who know the contraceptive method of all the women in their charge, and they watch for signs of pregnancy. If a woman accidentally or deliberately becomes pregnant a second time, she is subjected to 'ideological education'. This is a euphemism for being harangued and bullied into having an abortion.

In an article in the *Wall Street Journal* of 25th July 1983, Steven W. Mosher describes a stay of several months in a village in Guandong province of China. He writes of his horror at one effect of this one-child policy – infanticide of girl babies. Denied by population experts, there is no doubt that it occurs because the *Chinese People's Daily* on March 3, 1983, admitted that the 'butchering, drowning and leaving to die of female infants, and the maltreating of women who have given birth to girls, has become a grave social problem'. He quotes also the English language *Peking Review*, which said: 'In their keen desire to have sons, some men still torment their wives who have daughters, and worse still they kill the baby girls through neglect or outright murder'.

Families who actually have a second child must pay heavy fines of around £3,000, which is several years wages in mainland China. 'Not only are forced abortions being performed up to the time of birth, there are cases of legally-sanctioned infanticide'. He then goes on to describe how in his village a woman in her first pregnancy gave birth to twin boys. One of the babies – the mother could not and would not choose – was taken from her and killed. An unpleasant postscript to the awful story of Chinese methods of population control is its acceptance and even welcome by family-planning organisations in the west. Speakers at a conference in San Diego, of American Planned Parenthood, praised Communist China as 'the only country that has come to grips with the population problem'. Any suggestion that financial assistance should be withheld was called arrogant, and the conference was told that 'the United States should respect China's decision'.

I have written at length about the myth of over-population because I believe it is one aspect of an anti-child philosophy that perpetuates abortion and infanticide. I believe all three are bound together in an unholy alliance. It is a fact that most people involved with contraception in the underdeveloped world, believe it is vital to have easily available abortion as a 'back-up' when contraception fails.

The anti-life philosophy alters the whole attitude of a nation to its children. They are regarded not as the fruit of love or as a gift from God, but as optional extras allowed to be born if they come at a convenient time, and got rid of if they don't. The over-population myth is also responsible for a change in people's attitude to the handicapped. If population must decrease, the handicapped are the first to go. I have before me an article from the *American Journal of Rehabilitation*, titled 'Life-Boat Counselling: the issue of survival decisions'. It describes a course for graduates and one of the questions was – 'You are a rehabilitation counsellor living in the year 2001. You have just been informed that the world government has decreed that the earth is over-populated relative to its resources. It has therefore been decided that some people must be eliminated and that a priority listing must be made for that purpose. Since the government values the opinion of social and behavioural scientists, you have been invited to rank-order the disabilities listed on the board in order of expendibility'.

This was no joke, neither was it purely an academic exercise. The writer of the article says: 'Exercises of this kind could help rehabilitation professionals to begin to think through the issues involved, and the criteria to be used if life decisions should ever have to be made'. Throughout there is no suggestion that there is anything untoward in a Rehabilitation Professional picking out various handicapped people to be killed. It is an assumption certain people have made before . . .

I pray that this sort of thinking will never be put to effect again, and in that I have the backing of all the doctors who supported the Geneva Convention and, I hope, most in the medical profession today. But the philosophy that cheapens human life isn't accepted wholesale overnight. People will adopt it if they fear something else more – like a population explosion – and if they have already been softened up by a permissive attitude to apparently lesser issues. Abortion is not just an evil in itself (though it is indeed a very great evil), it is the herald of things far worse, a Trojan Horse. Let us be on our guard before accepting it.

8

Abortion and Modern Trends

> 'Then shall they also answer him saying – "Lord, when saw we thee anhungered or athirst, or a stranger or naked or sick or in prison and did not minister unto thee?" Then shall he answer unto them, saying – "Verily I say unto you, inasmuch as ye did it not to one of the least of these, ye did it not to me" ' *Matthew 25: 44–45*

We live in an age of powerful means but very confused ends. The American National Abortion Federation held its ninth annual meeting at the Westin Hotel, Boston, in June 1985. The theme was 'Abortion – a Moral Choice'. A report on the conference shows they were both rich and powerful in their means, but their ends seemed terribly confused. A clergy panel studied 'Abortion as a Moral Good'. The Revd. Ann Fowler, an Episcopal priest, was reported as saying that 'to deny women the right to abortion would be to commit the sin of sexism in a flagrant form'. Another woman, Ms Carter Hayward, who was ordained by the Episcopal Church in 1974, was reported as saying, 'if women had made the rules, if women had written the sacred texts, if women had been the architects of religion and state, sexuality would be understood as sacramental. So too would the act of love-making, whether heterosexual or homosexual – so too would conception, miscarrying and birth'. She went on, 'Abortion would be a sacrament if women were in charge ... an occasion of deep and serious and sacred meaning'. I wonder how a member of the clergy is able to reconcile this attitude, which to me is blasphemy, with their religious duties and their reading of the word of God. I believe the fundamental error lies in the totally false belief that everyone is entitled to everything they want and that heaven is a materialistic worldly Utopia.

The roots of this heresy in Britain lie in the depression and poverty of the thirties, followed closely by the deprivation of World War II which entailed rationing of food, clothes and heating. Not surprisingly, when the war was over, parents felt that they would try and ensure that their children did not suffer in the same way. This completely laudable intention had disastrous effects in some cases. I remember in the nineteen-sixties a mother bringing a three year old child to see me, with a luxurious doll's pram which contained two extremely expensive dolls. I knew the family had well below the average income, and I made a comment about the lavishness of the child's toys, to which she made a reply I have never forgotten. In fact, in that reply lie the seeds of the whole 'permissive' society. She said, 'Her Dad says, if she wants it, she's to have it'. It is not necessary for me to report what happened to that child – she caused continuous trouble at school, appeared at the Juvenile Court, became promiscuous and had an abortion before she discovered that in this life we can't have everything we want, and we wouldn't be happy if we could! It was Robert Browning, the great Christian poet, who wrote, 'But a man's reach must exceed his grasp, or what's a heaven for?'

The Modern Religion of Hedonism

Despite a profoundly Christian history, the prevailing religion of the west is hedonism. Instead of the population going to church on a Sunday to worship God, they are all out in front of their houses worshipping their new gods – possessions such as cars and boats, and leisure itself. In turn, because possessions have become the new gods, people do not want to *wait* for them and so we have hire-purchase and credit cards. It is the child who says, 'I want it and I want it now'. It is the mature person who can say, 'I want it but I'm not going to spoil it by grabbing, I shall wait till I have earned it'. The world is therefore divided into two sorts of people, those who demand instant gratification and those who are prepared to wait and accept deferred gratification. This impatient and immature attitude which applies to material gain is also applied to sexual experience. Why wait? Why not experience as much as possible *now?* The tragic belief that everyone has a right to sexual gratification as and when they choose, is one of the causes of the increase in abortion and sexually transmitted diseases.

Very few people are able to have everything they want in the way of material possessions, which is lucky for them, because there is no pleasure at all in vast wealth. Those who possess everything, value nothing. Half the fun of possession is the saving up and anticipation. G K Chesterton said, 'When people stop believing in God, they don't believe nothing, they'll believe anything!' And so we have quite intelligent people who actually believe that true happiness lies in material possessions. There are many glossy magazines which perpetuate this myth. They are full of articles about expensive clothes and houses, and may devote two whole pages to horoscopes! They barely mention Christianity, but genuflect to the primitive religion of astrology. Rich and successful pop groups and film stars fly off to the Orient to sit at the feet of Indian 'gurus', because they have discovered that materialism is a false god – and yet all they needed could have been found on their doorstep. As Francis Thompson put it poetically:

The angels keep their ancient places –
Turn but a stone and start a wing!
'Tis ye, 'tis your estranged faces
That miss the many-splendoured thing.

119

But when so sad thou canst not sadder
Cry; – and upon thy so sore loss,
Shall shine the traffic of Jacob's ladder
Pitched betwixt Heaven and Charing Cross.

Yea in the night my Soul my daughter
Cry – clinging heaven by the hems;
And lo, Christ walketh on the water
Not of Gennesareth but Thames.

The only true happiness comes from relationships with God and with our fellow men, and nothing, not all the tea in China nor all the automobiles in Detroit, can make up for a life that lacks love.

Our credit cards 'take the waiting out of wanting', so we can get material possessions with ease, but there seems to be evidence that this attitude spills over into the area of moral choices. In spite of the fact that opinion polls show that eighty-four per cent of girls in Britain want to be virgins when they get married, they are losing their virginity at a younger and younger age. Taking the waiting out of wanting has resulted in a situation where some young people (mainly men) have 'had it all' before they are twenty. They've worked through everything that was ever advertised in the colour supplements. They've had everything (so they imagine). What they have actually had is everything they want, but nothing they need. The realisation that the world has sold them only fools' gold, caused many of our cleverest young people to drop out of society. They felt they had been let down by life; in fact they'd never even *tried* it.

Where does abortion come into all this? Sex is one of the pleasures that young people expect to enjoy as their right at a younger and younger age. Unfortunately no one has told them that sexual intercourse is not just a matter of physical copulation – it is of course possible to enjoy sex for kicks (though girls should realise that sometimes when a boy says

'I love you' he actually means 'I love me and I want you'), but this bears little relationship with sexual intercourse between husband and wife, which is sex for commitment. This is an ecstatic experience only partly physical, a total giving. Abortion goes hand in hand with second-class sex; it is considered and demanded as a 'back-up' to contraception.

I have described many of the side-effects of abortion, both mental and physical – one especially fits in here. Abortion often breaks up a relationship. If you can kill the child in the womb who is the fruit of your love, you will end up killing your love. Perhaps not at once; it may take ten years but it's almost inevitable in the end. I remember a beautiful woman who had an abortion because her husband insisted. She didn't want to, but she told me with tears in her eyes – 'I did it to save my marriage'. Her husband left her a few months later. There is one exception to this rule and that is true repentance and receiving absolution from above. In these cases husband and wife can experience a new life together in God's light.

In the United States there is an organisation called 'Foundation Rachel' which, through counselling and reconciliation with God, brings peace to women who are suffering because they can't forgive themselves for taking the life of their child. It is called 'Foundation Rachel' because of the description in the Bible of the massacre of the innocents:

'Then Herod when he saw that he was mocked of the wise men, was exceeding wroth and sent forth and slew all the children that were in Bethlehem and in all the coasts thereof from two years old and under, according to the time that he had diligently enquired of the wise men. Then was fulfilled that which was spoken by Jeremiah the prophet, saying: In Rama was there a voice heard, lamentation and weeping and great mourning. Rachel weeping for her children and would not be comforted, because they are not'. *Matthew 2. 16.*

121

I believe our materialistic society is making the primary error of turning people into 'things', so *people* are used and *objects* are loved. We are not loving our neighbour as ourselves and using our microwave oven, but exactly the reverse; using our neighbour and loving our microwave.

I have felt for a long time that some pro-absortionists had fascist tendencies and the feeling is confirmed in Dr. and Mrs. J. Willke's latest book *Abortion, Question and Answers*. They report that in the USA, there have been two minority race babies killed by abortion for every one white baby. Erma Clardy Craven, a beautiful black pro-life social worker, described a case where a middle-class girl in her teens became pregnant and all arrangements were made for her to have the baby and get it adopted until she told her parents the father was black – then she was pressured into having an abortion. I mentioned these facts when speaking at a pro-life meeting in America. I pointed out that discrimination tends to be indivisible, and if you are prepared to discriminate on the grounds of size, and sex (in countries which permit abortion where the child is not of the required sex – three baby girls are killed in the womb for every boy), it won't be long before racial discrimination rears its ugly head. I was attacked in a medical magazine for suggesting that such a thing could be possible. One sentence ran – 'Dr. White seems to imply that any attempt to advise a woman happening to have a black skin *to contain socially undesirable fecundity is genocide'* (emphasis mine). The phrase 'socially undesirable fecundity' is a euphemism, it's also a 'give-away', what it means is 'these people are socially unfit to breed as they wish', and is an example of the very sort of discrimination I was deploring.

It's tough to be pro-life!

The vast majority of the general public in western countries tend to be ineffective in the abortion debate, disapproving of easily-obtainable abortion, but browbeaten by the media into believing they should not attempt to 'moralise'. It takes a lot of courage to stand up for the imperfect and unwanted, not everyone has a tough enough skin to take the taunts and insults that come as part of the package deal when you run up a pro-life flag. God has bestowed on me the hide of a rhinocerous, most of the time when people are insulting me, I don't even realise it! Needless to say, one occasion when I definitely did feel the insult was when, during a TV debate I was accused in a most unpleasant manner of being frigid because I was opposed to abortion! 'Frigidity' is today's all-purpose insult. As it was quite impossible to prove on stage in front of the television cameras in a few minutes, that I was not frigid, I decided to accept the insult as just another battle scar and concentrate on the unborn child.

Compared with the general apathy about the wholesale killing of the child in the womb, the value that the west places on all forms of animal life is vastly out of proportion. No organisations are better endowed and supported than those which protest against the killing of whales or the hunting of hares. A young girl who worked in a restaurant was fined for 'cruelty to prawns', and as one of our best comedians said in a television show – 'When you see people coming out of a cinema weeping, you know that Lassie has cut her paw again'. In America it is possible to be fined $500 for stealing an iguana egg! This shows how crazy modern attitudes are. If you kill an unborn ugly lizard you are punished, but you are permitted to kill an unborn human being. If 470 baby rabbits were killed each day instead of 470 unborn babies, there would be riots in the streets. If abbatoirs killed sheep and cattle as painfully as the unborn is killed, the law would be changed within weeks. For some strange reason animals enjoy many privileges denied to the unborn baby.

123

The Women's Movement and Abortion

The effect of abortion on demand on western society has been much more widespread than could have been imagined, it has turned society and even people who have not, and would not have an abortion, from child-lovers to child-tolerators. It is rather a paradox that the Women's Movement which was supposed to make life better for woman, has with few exceptions made life worse. Because women have been exhorted to be equal to men, the most wonderful job of all – wife and mother – has become so undervalued that those women who do not work outside the home feel constrained to apologise when asked what they do, and so it is common to hear people say – 'I'm afraid I'm only a housewife'. The Women's Liberation Movement, in its misguided efforts to improve the lives of women, has in many cases made it harder. True equality of the sexes will only come when women can become pregnant and still be considered 'equal', when being a housewife and mother is not something to apologise for but something to be proud of, because you know that your role is an honoured one and the work that you do is probably more important than any other. Because unborn life has become cheap and disposable the attitude of parents to their exhisting children has changed. The Women's Movement has always maintained that those children that we *do* permit to be born will be healthier, wealthier, and, much more important, that new breed of offspring so dear to the heart of the humanists 'the wanted child'. Like nearly all their other predictions, this one too has turned out to be false. Dr. Ney of Victoria BC, a professor of Psychological Medicine, in a superb article published in an edition of *Child and Family* (Vol. 19, No.2) writes, 'With the increasing number of abortions by choice, there should be an increased number of women who really wanted their children. On the contrary there appears to be an increased number of people who would rather not have kids'.

The Women's Movement which was founded to deliver women from the bondage of the kitchen and children, has succeeded only too well. It is not surprising there is a demand for Sunday opening of shops – with a full-time job it's difficult for a woman to do her shopping in the week. In fact it is difficult for women to find time for lots of things in today's society. They must dress well, wear the right perfume and read the right magazines, and so have no time to enjoy the most precious aspects of parenthood. The victory of the movement to liberate women has brought them a trophy of nothing but 'dead sea fruit'. They now have the privilege of going out to work all day *and* doing the housework in the evening *and* clean the carpets and do the ironing at the weekends. There was a time when it didn't matter if a woman looked as though she'd just got up from scrubbing the floor when a neighbour called, the pressure now from women's magazines is for women to be groomed and chic at all times. Most women find complete fulfilment in obtaining the highly honourable job of wife and mother – it is not surprising because that was the plan for them made by nature, and nature is a better planner than politicians.

Abortion and the Handicapped

Abortion, as well as affecting people's attitude to babies, has also affected their attitude to the handicapped. It is considered perfectly proper to do a late abortion in these cases (it is not possible to discover if the child is handicapped before about twenty weeks). Late abortions are more unpleasant for both the mother and the abortionist, but it is considered necessary for them both to endure this unpleasantness rather than permit the birth of a child that is different from the rest of us. It is hard to imagine the effect of this attitude on the handicapped themselves. Any handicapped person born before the abortion act must face the fact that had they been conceived today they may not have

125

been allowed to live beyond a few months in the womb. Added to their natural distress at being different is the feeling that the 'normal' population feel they ought not to have been born. This feeling of rejection is augmented when they read that a well-known pro-abortionist has complained of pictures printed in the press showing Thalidomide children laughing! We are back to the evil heresy that our 'quality of life' depends on our physical appearance and intelligence quotient. This is latter day eugenics, which teaches the handicapped should not be allowed to 'pollute' our world, and because this neo-nazism is camouflaged as concern for these abnormal people with their poor quality of life, we must not be shown pictures which demonstrate that even without arms the Thalidomide children can enjoy life.

I once heard a lecture by a worker with Downs children. He told us that his adolescent Downs daughter watched a programme on television about the use of amniocentesis to discover if a woman was carrying a handicapped child. When it was over she said, 'Daddy, they would have killed me if they had known'. He reassured her that he would have protected her. A few minutes later she turned round suddenly and asked, 'Daddy, do they want to kill me now?'

9

The Still Small Voice of Calm

'I call heaven and earth to record this day against you, that I have set before you life and death, blessing and cursing. Therefore choose life, that both thou and thy seed may live'. *Deuteronomy 30. 19*

Dorothy Thompson, the eminent American journalist, said, when writing on the lesson of Dachau, 'I'm beginning to think that when God goes, all goes'. She was echoing the saying 'If God is not, nothing is wrong'. If there is 'no divinity that shapes our ends' there can be no absolute right and absolute wrong; what is good in one generation becomes bad in the next because there is no solid rock on which to build our moral code. I remember being told at my school that a very important yardstick was kept at a certain temperature in a special case, so that alterations in temperature or humidity would not make it shrink or stretch – this way we were able, by checking against the yardstick, to make sure that over the decades a yard remained the same length. In other words we need a criterion: if we have no criteria which we know is right, we live a life of confusia and uncertainty. Why should we maintain a commitment to being morally good if we do not have a vision of what is possible? Faith, that is, a belief in a God who is unchanging, and a criteria against which we can check when our actions are in doubt is vital to the moral life.

Can We Rely on the Law?

If we have no God by whom to check our behaviour, we'll accept the dictates of the law. The law may be good or it may be bad, it is most unlikely in the twentieth century that it will enshrine Christian morality. However, although there is no law in the world that can make us do what is good, there are, tragically, many laws that facilitate wrong behaviour. The law is a great teacher. A child knows that the National Health Service arranged special baby clinics where she received care and immunisation against disease, and special school clinics to check her eyesight and hearing. If she discovers the same doctors are running special clinics where girls from twelve years old upward may go and be provided with free and secret contraception, she will naturally assume that such clinics must be for the good of her health. In the same way, when the doctors in these clinics refer young girls for abortion, the children assume it is the best possible solution for their problem, otherwise these trustworthy doctors wouldn't arrange it for them. So we are rearing a generation of children who accept the law as the arbiter of good and moral behaviour. Probably the root of the problem lies in the deliberate and successful attempt by the moral anarchists to separate the sexual act from both commitment, reproduction and even love. 'Sex for kicks' is the message received by many of our immature adolescents. The fact that contraception is both free and behind their parents' backs, has not stopped these unfortunate and misled children becoming pregnant. In 1983, 5.38 children out of every thousand children aged thirteen to fifteen, had abortions before their sixteenth birthday. In 1969 the rate was only 1.7. The dissociation of sexual intercourse from reproduction and marital commitment, has caused a complete change in the attitude of the young to babies. Children are a gift from God and the fruit of a loving relationship, but today's prevailing philosophy teaches that pleasure is king and if the conception of a child interferes with that pleasure, the child must be aborted.

The Bible says very little directly about abortion, but many times it makes clear that after conception a new life comes into being – a unique if infinitesimal part of God's creation.

'I will praise thee, for I am fearfully and wonderfully made. Marvellous are thy works, and that my soul knoweth right well. My substance was not hid from thee when I was made in secret and curiously wrought in the lowest parts of the earth.

Thine eyes did see my substance, yet being unperfect and in thy book all my members were written, which in continuance were fashioned, when as yet there were none of them'. *Psalm 139 verses 14 – 16*

It is perfectly clear from these verses that God accepts the unborn child as an individual. Perhaps the clearest evidence of God's attitude to the unborn, comes in the Book of the Prophet Jeremiah (Chapter 1, verse 5) 'Before I formed thee in the belly I knew thee; and before thou camest forth out of the womb I sanctified thee, and I ordained thee a prophet unto the nations'.

I believe that it is relatively easy for an atheist to believe in abortion on demand – if you do not believe that God has made man in his own image and loves us as His children, there is less reason to suppose you should care about your fellow man, born or unborn. Needless to say, what is tragic is to find *Christians* of all denominations who accept that abortion is a valid option at least when pregnancies prove problematic.

Professor Duncan Vere, consulting physician to the London Hospital, writing in the journal of the Christian Medical Fellowship, makes a very interesting point – 'Now it seems that when our brothers are saying that passages like Psalm 139 and Jeremiah 1 and many like them, "show" that

129

embryos have fully human status as persons, they cannot argue this as what must follow from those passages of necessity (i.e. by deduction), but rather that the sense of scripture as a whole suggests that paramount respect is due even to these earliest forms of human life. After all, it would seem bizarre were God believed to hold a strong personal interest and care over two adults as persons, then to withhold that interest from their newly-fertilised ovum, only to renew it again at its implantation, innervation, vascularisation, quickening or birth'.

There is no definite law laid down on abortion in the Bible, but the whole attitude of scripture makes it clear that our duty is always to protect the weak, the sick and the unwanted. I have little doubt that the life of a leper in Palestine in the first century AD was pretty horrible, but when confronted by lepers Jesus did not say – 'You poor things, what a dreadful quality of life you have, and it will be even worse when you are old, therefore I will kill you (painlessly of course, because I am compassionate)'. And yet there are Christian clergy who were prepared to say that it is an act of Christian charity to kill a new born child because he has Downs syndrome.

Over the years I have come to realise that the question of abortion and infanticide is the acid test of true Christianity. Those who support abortion will always wrap up their reasons for this support in layer after layer of euphemisms. I have heard it said, 'I don't agree with abortion, but we have to face facts as they are, and I would support any woman who, after considerable thought made the agonising decision ["agonising decision" is a euphemism which is scattered around like confetti outside a church on Saturday] that her pregnancy should be terminated because. . . .' Then follows a whole series of reasons varying from interference with her studies or career, to being behind with the mortgage payments. Not surprisingly those clergy who are prepared to accept this killing of the weakest and most innocent of God's creatures, are often those who have doubts about the Virgin Birth and bodily resurrection of Our Lord. Those who believe and accept the faith of their fathers rarely compromise their beliefs to fit with the prevailing public opinion of the day. They know that those who are married to the philosophy and morals of this generation will be widowed in the next. It is hard to 'kick against the pricks' but the church has always known that it must be prepared to be unpopular and even derided. It has to be said that if the church is too popular, the odds are that it's not doing its job properly. The church has always been in the forefront of the fight for freedom, it has fought against slavery, against serfdom, for children, the sick and the old, in short for all, not just the rich. How can the church opt out of the fight to stop the mass killing of the unborn? The right to education, a vote, good housing and health care are useless without the primary and all-important right – the right to life itself. I refuse to accept the absurd excuse that killing the unborn, unwanted or handicapped is done in the name of justice, humanity and compassion. Malcolm Muggeridge said 'Almost all the evil things that have been done in the world in the last decades, have been done in the name of justice, equality, and compassion'.

However, not all is gloom – thanks to the original tiny band of people who refused to accept that abortion was one form of contraception, there is now a huge worldwide army of pro-lifers, which grows every day. The most exciting thing about the pro-life movement is that our greatest support is among the young. There are pro-life groups in all universities and most schools, and the wind of change is blowing pro-life. This generation of students are probably more concerned and caring of the underdog than past generations, and they can see the hypocrisy of demanding greater child allowances and better education for infants, while at the same time supporting the mass killing of their brothers and sisters.

In many ways there are signs of hope. Darwinism has

131

finally been discarded by all but a few scientists, because since computers were developed it has been realised that the haphazard development of humans from primordial slime is mathematically impossible. The move is towards holistic medicine and away from high technology and from situations where the doctor scarcely speaks to the patient, but makes diagnoses and determines treatment from more and ever more complicated tests. Doctors are realising more and more that health is associated with all sorts of extraordinarily unscientific things, like whether you have a running feud with your mother-in-law or next-door neighbour. We are, after all, 'fearfully and wonderfully made'.

The duty of a Christian in the present abortion situation is twofold – firstly, to do everything in his power to get the law of the land altered to protect all of God's children. This means writing letters to the press, to radio and television and to Members of Parliament who make the laws. Secondly it means not being afraid to speak up among friends and workmates when the subject comes up, it means joining one of the many pro-life organisations and working together with others to get the law changed. For over two thousand years since the time of the Old Testament, people have feared the locust, still today it strikes terror into the hearts of farmers in parts of the world, because of its devastating effect on the crops and upon all growing vegetation. But what is this scourge which we have feared for thousands of years? It's nothing but a grasshopper! But the valuable lesson we can learn from this creature is the way it has learnt to work together with all its friends and relations instead of 'going it alone'. I suggest we strengthen our voice by joining together with others who abhor death before birth.

Christians have a second duty which cannot be neglected. It is vital that they run pregnancy aid services where unhappy and perplexed women may go and receive information about the help they can obtain from the state or voluntary bodies (about, for instance, having their child adopted). If necessary

Christians can also help in providing homes for pregnant girls who may have unsympathetic or uncaring families. We are, in this country, well endowed with Christian organisations to help the unmarried mother and her child, but those of us who speak up for the right to life must be prepared to help the pregnancy aid services and if necessary we must take the pregnant woman into our own homes. This work is very important, but the prime object must also be an alteration in the law; otherwise we are merely mopping up the water flowing over the side of a brimming bath without bothering to turn off the taps. Mopping up the floor is important but turning off the taps is vital!

It is a difficult and sometimes lonely path we tread, but every year it gets less so. No more are we able to 'walk by on the other side' and leave the bruised and battered bodies of unborn children to be burned in the hospital incinerators. Churchill said, many years ago, something which has often given me strength to carry on when everything has seemed utterly hopeless and I began to think, 'Why should I bother, it's no good, why not just quit the fight and cultivate my roses?' He said, 'When you know you are right you must never, never, NEVER give up'.

John Donne in 1631 wrote these famous lines: 'No man is an island entire of itself; every man is a piece of the continent, a part of the main; if a clod be washed away by the sea, Europe is the less, as well as if a promontory were, as well as if a manor of thy friends or thy own were. Everyman's death diminishes me, because I am involved in mankind; and therefore never send to know for whom the bell tolls; it tolls for thee'. God grant that we never grow insensitive to its tolling.

'My son, keep thy father's commandment, and forsake not the law of thy mother, bind them continually upon thine heart, and tie them about thy neck. When thou goest it shall lead thee; when thou sleepest it shall keep thee; and when thou wakest it shall talk with thee. For the commandment is a lamp and the law is light'. *Proverbs 6. 20 – 23*

If you wish to receive *regular information* about *new books,* please send your name and address to:

London Bible Warehouse
PO Box 123
Basingstoke
Hants RG23 7NL

Name...

Address...

....

....

....

 I am especially interested in:
☐ Biographies
☐ Fiction
☐ Christian living
☐ Issue related books
☐ Academic books
☐ Bible study aids
☐ Children's books
☐ Music
☐ Other subjects

P.S. If you have ideas for new Christian Books or other products, please write to us too!